New Comedies

Lady Gregory

Alpha Editions

This edition published in 2022

ISBN: 9789356713222

Design and Setting By

Alpha Editions
www.alphaedis.com

Email - info@alphaedis.com

Contents

THE BOGIE MEN

Scene: A Shed near where a coach stops. Darby comes in. Has a tin can of water in one hand, a sweep's bag and brush in the other. He lays down bag on an empty box and puts can on the floor. Is taking a showy suit of clothes out of bag and admiring them and is about to put them on when he hears some one coming and hurriedly puts them back into the bag.

Taig: (At door.) God save all here!

Darby: God save you. A sweep is it? *(Suspiciously.)* What brought you following me?

Taig: Why wouldn't I be a sweep as good as yourself?

Darby: It is not one of my own trade I came looking to meet with. It is a shelter I was searching out, where I could put on a decent appearance, rinsing my head and my features in a tin can of water.

Taig: Is it long till the coach will be passing by the cross-road beyond?

Darby: Within about a half an hour they were telling me.

Taig: There does be much people travelling to this place?

Darby: I suppose there might, and it being the high road from the town of Ennis.

Taig: It should be in this town you follow your trade?

Darby: It is not in the towns I do be.

Taig: There's nothing but the towns, since the farmers in the country clear out their own chimneys with a bush under and a bush overhead.

Darby: I travel only gentlemen's houses.

Taig: There does be more of company in the streets than you'd find on the bare road.

Darby: It isn't easy get company for a person has but two empty hands.

Taig: Wealth to be in the family it is all one nearly with having a grip of it in your own palm.

Darby: I wish to the Lord it was the one thing.

Taig: You to know what I know—

Darby: What is it that you know?

Taig: It is dealing out cards through the night time I will be from this out, and making bets on racehorses and fighting-cocks through all the hours of the day.

Darby: I would sooner to be sleeping in feathers and to do no hand's turn at all, day or night.

Taig: If I came paddling along through every place this day and the road hard under my feet, it is likely I will have my choice way leaving it.

Darby: How is that now?

Taig: A horse maybe and a car or two horses, or maybe to go in the coach, and I myself sitting alongside the man came in it.

Darby: Is it that he is taking you into his service?

Taig: Not at all! And I being of his own family and his blood.

Darby: Of his blood now?

Taig: A relation I have, that is full up of money and of every whole thing.

Darby: A relation?

Taig: A first cousin, by the side of the mother.

Darby: Well, I am not without having a first cousin of my own.

Taig: I wouldn't think he'd be much. To be listening to my mother giving out a report of my one's ways, you would maybe believe it is no empty skin of a man he is.

Darby: My own mother was not without giving out a report of my man's ways.

Taig: Did she see him?

Darby: She did, I suppose, or the thing was near him. She never was tired talking of him.

Taig: It is often my own mother would have Dermot pictured to myself.

Darby: It is often the likeness of Timothy was laid down to me by the teaching of my mother's mouth, since I was able to walk the floor. She thought the whole world of him.

Taig: A bright scholar she laid Dermot down to be. A good doing fellow for himself. A man would be well able to go up to his promise.

Darby: That is the same account used to be given out of Timothy.

Taig: To some trade of merchandise it is likely Dermot was reared. A good living man that was never any cost on his mother.

Darby: To own an estate before he would go far in age Timothy was on the road.

Taig: To have the handling of silks and jewelleries and to be free of them, and of suits and the making of suits, that is the way with the big merchants of the world.

Darby: It is letting out his land to grass farmers a man owning acres does be making his profit.

Taig: A queer thing you to be the way you are, and he to be an upstanding gentleman.

Darby: It is the way I went down; my mother used to be faulting me and I not being the equal of him. Tormenting and picking at me and shouting me on the road. "You thraneen," she'd say, "you little trifle of a son! You stumbling over the threshold as if in slumber, and Timothy being as swift as a bee!"

Taig: So my own mother used to be going on at myself, and be letting out shrieks and screeches. "What now would your cousin Dermot be saying?" every time there would come a new rent in my rags.

Darby: "Little he'd think of you," she'd say; "you without body and puny, not fit to lift scraws from off the field, and Timothy bringing in profit to his mother's hand, and earning prizes and rewards."

Taig: The time it would fail me to follow my book or to say off my A, B, ab, to draw Dermot down on me she would. "Before he was up to your age," she would lay down, "he was fitted to say off Catechisms and to read newses. You have no more intellect beside him," she'd say, "than a chicken has its head yet in the shell."

Darby: "Let you hold up the same as Timothy," she'd give out, and I to stoop my shoulders the time the sun would prey upon my head. "He that is as straight and as clean as a green rush on the brink of the bog."

Taig: "It is you will be fit but to blow the bellows," my mother would say, "the time Dermot will be forging gold." I let on the book to have gone astray on me at the last. Why would I go crush and bruise myself under a weight of learning, and there being one in the family well able to take my cost and my support whatever way it might go? Dermot that would feel my keep no more than the lake would feel the weight of the duck.

Darby: I seen no use to be going sweating after farmers, striving to plough or to scatter seed, when I never could come anear Timothy in any sort of a way, and he, by what she was saying, able to thrash out a rick of oats in the day. So it fell out I was thrown on the ways of the world, having no skill in any trade, till there came a demand for me going aloft in chimneys, I being as thin as a needle and shrunken with weakness and want of food.

Taig: I got my living for a while by miracle and trafficking in rabbit skins, till a sweep from Limerick bound me to himself one time I was skinned with the winter. Great cruelty he gave me till I ran from him with the brush and the bag, and went foraging around for myself.

Darby: So am I going around by myself. I never had a comrade lad.

Taig: My mother that would hit me a crack if I made free with any of the chaps of the village, saying that would not serve me with Dermot, that had a good top-coat and was brought up to manners and behaviour.

Darby: My own mother that drew down Timothy on me the time she'd catch me going with the lads that had their pleasure out of the world, slashing tops and pebbles, throwing and going on with games.

Taig: I took my own way after, fitting myself for sports and funning, against the time the rich man would stretch out his hand. Going with wild lads and poachers I was, till they left me carrying their snares in under my coat, that I was lodged for three months in the gaol.

Darby: The neighbours had it against me after, I not being friendly when we were small. The most time I am going the road it is a lonesome shadow I cast before me.

Taig: (Looking out of the door.) It is on this day I will be making acquaintance with himself. My mother that sent him a request to come meet me in this town on this day, it being the first of the summer.

Darby: My own mother that did no less, telling me she got word from Timothy he would come meet here with myself. It is certain he will bring me into his house, she having wedded secondly with a labouring man has got a job at Golden Hill in Lancashire. I would not recognise him beyond any other one.

Taig: I would recognise the signs of a big man. I wish I was within in his kitchen. There is a pinch of hunger within in my heart.

Darby: So there is within in myself.

Taig: Is there nothing at all in the bag?

Darby: It is a bit of a salted herring.

Taig: Why wouldn't you use it?

Darby: I would be delicate coming before him and the smell of it to be on me, and all the grand meats will be at his table.

Taig: (Showing a bottle.) The full of a pint I have of porter, that fell from a tinker's car.

Darby: I wonder you would not swallow it down for to keep courage in your mind.

Taig: It is what I am thinking, I to take it fasting, it might put confusion and wildness in my head. I would wish, and I meeting with him, my wits to be of the one clearness with his own. It is not long to be waiting; it is in claret I will be quenching my thirst to-night, or in punch!

Darby: (Looking out.) I am nearly in dread meeting Timothy, fearing I will not be pleasing to him, and I not acquainted with his habits.

Taig: I would not be afeard, and Dermot to come sparkling in, and seven horses in his coach.

Darby: What way can I come before him at all? I would be better pleased you to personate me and to stand up to him in my place.

Taig: Any person to put orders on me, or to bid me change my habits, I'd give no heed! I'd stand up to him in the spite of his teeth!

Darby: If it wasn't for the hearthfires to be slackened with the springtime, and my work to be lessened with the strengthening of the sun, I'd sooner not see him till another moon is passed, or two moons.

Taig: He to bid me read out the news of the world, taking me to be a scholar, I'd give him words that are in no books! I'd give him newses! I'd knock rights out of him or any one I ever seen.

Darby: I could speak only of my trade. The boundaries of the world to be between us, I'm thinking I'd never ask to go cross them at all.

Taig: He to go into Court swearing witnesses and to bring me along with him to face the judges and the whole troop of the police, I'd go bail I'll be no way daunted or scared.

Darby: What way can I keep company with him? I that was partly reared in the workhouse. And he having a star on his hat and a golden apple in his hand. He will maybe be bidding me to scour myself with soapy water all the Sundays and Holy days of the year! I tell you I am getting low hearted. I pray to the Lord to forgive me where I did not go under the schoolmaster's rod!

Taig: I that will shape crampy words the same as any scholar at all! I'll let on to be a master of learning and of Latin!

Darby: Ah, what letting on? It is Timothy will look through me the same as if my eyes were windows, and my thoughts standing as plain as cattle under the risen sun! It is easier letting on to have knowledge than to put on manners and behaviour.

Taig: Ah, what's manners but to refuse no man a share of your bite and to keep back your hand from throwing stones?

Darby: I tell you I'm in shivers! My heart that is shaking like an ivy leaf! My bones that are loosened and slackened in the similitude of a rope of tow! I'd sooner meet with a lion of the wilderness or the wickedest wind of the hills! I thought it never would come to pass. I'd sooner go into the pettiest house, the wildest home and the worst! Look at here now. Let me stop along with yourself. I never let out so much of my heart to any one at all till this day. It's a pity we should be parted!

Taig: Is it to come following after me you would, before the face of Dermot?

Darby: I'd feel no dread and you being at my side.

Taig: Dermot to see me in company with the like of you! I wouldn't for the whole world he should be aware I had ever any traffic with chimneys or with soot. It would not be for his honour you to draw anear him!

Darby: (Indignantly.) No but Timothy that would make objection to yourself! He that would whip the world for manners and behaviour!

Taig: Dermot that is better again. He that would write and dictate to you at the one time!

Darby: What is that beside owning tillage, and to need no education, but to take rents into your hand?

Taig: I would never believe him to own an estate.

Darby: Why wouldn't he own it? "The biggest thing and the grandest," my mother would say when I would ask her what was he doing.

Taig: Ah, what could be before selling out silks and satins. There is many an estated lord couldn't reach you out a fourpenny bit.

Darby: The grandest house around the seas of Ireland he should have, beautifully made up! You would nearly go astray in it! It wouldn't be known what you could make of it at all! You wouldn't have it walked in a month!

Taig: What is that beside having a range of shops as wide maybe as the street beyond?

Darby: A house would be the capital of the county! One door for the rich, one door for the common! Velvet carpets rolled up, the way there would no dust from the chimney fall upon them. A hundred wouldn't be many standing in a corner of that place! A high bed of feathers, curled hair mattresses. A cover laid on it would be flowery with blossoms of gold!

Taig: Muslin and gauze, cambric and linen! Canton crossbar! Glass windows full up of ribbons as gaudy as the crooked bow in the sky! Sovereigns and shillings in and out as plenty as to riddle rape seed. Sure them that do be selling in shops die leaving millions.

Darby: Your man is not so good as mine in his office or in his billet.

Taig: There is the horn of the coach. Get out now till I'll prepare myself. He might chance to come seeking for me here.

Darby: There's a lather of sweat on myself. That's my tin can of water!

Taig: (Holding can from him.) Get out I tell you! I wouldn't wish him to feel the smell of you on the breeze.

Darby: (Almost crying.) You are a mean savage to go keeping from me my tin can and my rag!

Taig: Go wash yourself at the pump can't you?

Darby: That we may never be within the same four walls again, or come under the lintel of the one door! *(He goes out.)*

Taig: (Calling after him while he takes a suit of clothes from his bag.) I'm not like yourself! I have good clothes to put on me, what you haven't got! A body-coat my mother made out—she lost up to three shillings on it,—and a hat—and a speckled blue cravat. *(He hastily throws off his sweep's smock and cap, and puts on clothes. As he does he sings:)*

All round my hat I wore a green ribbon,
All round my hat for a year and a day;
And if any one asks me the reason I wore it
I'll say that my true love went over the sea!

All in my hat I will stick a blue feather
The same as the birds do be up in the tree;
And if you would ask me the reason I do it
I'll tell you my true love is come back to me!

(He washes his face and wipes it, looking at himself in the tin can. He catches sight of a straw hat passing window.)

Who is that? A gentleman? *(He draws back.)*

(Darby comes in. He has changed his clothes and wears a straw hat and light coat and trousers. He is looking for a necktie which he had dropped and picks up. His back is turned to Taig who is standing at the other door.)

Taig: (Awed.) It cannot be that you are Dermot Melody?

Darby: My father's name was Melody sure enough, till he lost his life in the year of the black potatoes.

Taig: It is yourself I am come here purposely to meet with.

Darby: You should be my mother's sister's son so, Timothy O'Harragha.

Taig: (Sheepishly.) I am that. I am sorry indeed it failed me to be out before you in the street.

Darby: Oh, I wouldn't be looking for that much from you.

(They are trying to keep their backs to each other, and to rub their faces cleaner.)

Taig: I wouldn't wish to be anyway troublesome to you. I am badly worthy of you.

Darby: It is in dread I am of being troublesome to yourself.

Taig: Oh, it would be hard for *you* to be that. Nothing you could put on me would be any hardship at all, if it was to walk steel thistles.

Darby: You have a willing heart surely.

Taig: Any little job at all I could do for you———

Darby: All I would ask of you is to give me my nourishment and my bite.

Taig: I will do that. I will be your serving man.

Darby: Ah, you are going too far in that.

Taig: It's my born duty to do that much. I'll bring your dinner before you, if I can be anyway pleasing to you; you that is used to wealthy people.

Darby: Indeed I was often in a house having up to twenty chimneys.

Taig: You are a rare good man, nothing short of it, and you going as you did so high in the world.

Darby: Any person would go high before he would put his hand out through the top of a chimney.

Taig: Having full and plenty of every good thing.

Darby: I saw nothing so plentiful as soot. There is not the equal of it nourishing a garden. It would turn every crop blue, being so good.

Taig: (Weeping.) It is a very unkind thing to go drawing chimneys down on me and soot, and you having all that ever was!

Darby: Little enough I have or ever had.

Taig: To be casting up my trade against me, I being poor and hungry, and you having coins and tokens from all the goldpits of the world.

Darby: I wish I ever handled a coin of gold in my lifetime.

Taig: To speak despisingly, not pitiful. And I thinking the chimney sweeping would be forgot and not reproached to me, if you have handled the fooleries and watches of the world, that you don't know the end of your riches!

Darby: I am maybe getting your meaning wrong, your tongue being a little hard and sharp because you are Englified, but I am without new learnments and so I speak flat.

Taig: You to have the millions of King Solomon, you have no right to be putting reflections on me! I would never behave that way, and housefuls to fall into my hand.

Darby: You are striving to put ridicule on me and to make a fool of me. That is a very unseemly thing to do! I that did not ask to go hide the bag or the brush.

Taig: There you are going on again. Is it to the customers in your shops you will be giving out that it was my lot to go through the world as a sweep?

Darby: Customers and shops! Will you stop your funning? Let you quit mocking and making a sport of me! That is very bad acting behaviour.

Taig: Striving to blacken my face again at the time I had it washed pure white. You surely have a heart of marble.

Darby: What way at all can you be putting such a rascally say out of your mouth? I'll take no more talk from you, I to be twenty-two degrees lower than the Hottentots!

Taig: If you are my full cousin Dermot Melody I'll make you quit talking of soot!

Darby: I'll take no more talk from yourself!

Taig: Have a care now!

Darby: Have a care yourself!

(Each gives the other a push. They stumble and fall, sitting facing one another. Darby's hat falls off.)

Taig: Is it *you* it is?

Darby: Who else would it be?

Taig: What call had you letting on to be Dermot Melody?

Darby: What letting on? Dermot is my full name, but Darby is the name I am called.

Taig: Are you a man owning riches and shops and merchandise?

Darby: I am not, or anything of the sort.

Taig: Have you teems of money in the bank?

Darby: If I had would I be sitting on this floor?

Taig: You thief you!

Darby: Thief yourself! Turn around now till I will measure your features and your face. *Yourself* is it! Is it personating my cousin Timothy you are?

Taig: I am personating no one but myself.

Darby: You letting on to be an estated magistrate and my own cousin and such a great generation of a man. And you not owning so much as a rood of ridges!

Taig: Covering yourself with choice clothing for to deceive me and to lead me astray!

Darby: Putting on your head a fine glossy hat and I thinking you to have come with the spring-tide, the way you had luck through your life!

Taig: Letting on to be Dermot Melody! You that are but the cull and the weakling of a race! It is a queer game you played on me and a crooked game. I never would have brought my legs so far to meet with the sooty likes of you!

Darby: Letting on to be my poor Timothy O'Harragha!

Taig: I never was called but Taig. Timothy was a sort of a Holy day name.

Darby: Where now are our two cousins? Or is it that the both of us are cracked?

Taig: It is, or our mothers before us.

Darby: My mother was a McGarrity woman from Loughrea. It is Mary was her Christened name.

Taig: So was my own mother of the McGarritys. It is sisters they were sure enough.

Darby: That makes us out to be full cousins in the heel.

Taig: You no better than myself! And the prayers I used to be saying for you, and you but a sketch and an excuse of a man!

Darby: Ah, I am thinking people put more in their prayers than was ever put in them by God.

Taig: Our mothers picturing us to one another as if we were the best in the world.

Darby: Lies I suppose they were drawing down, for to startle us into good behaviour.

Taig: Wouldn't you say now mothers to be a terror?

Darby: And we nothing at all after but two chimney sweepers and two harmless drifty lads.

Taig: Where is the great quality dinner yourself was to give me, having seven sorts of dressed meat? Pullets and bacon I was looking for, and to fall on an easy life.

Darby: Gone like the clouds of the winter's fog. We rose out of it the same as we went in.

Taig: We have nothing to do but to starve with the hunger, and you being as bare as myself.

Darby: We are in a bad shift surely. We must perish with the want of support. It is one of the tricks of the world does be played upon the children of Adam.

Taig: All we have to do is to crawl to the poorhouse gate. Or to go dig a pit in the graveyard, as it is short till we'll be stretched there with the want of food.

Darby: Food is it? There is nothing at this time against me eating my bit of a herring.

(Seizes it and takes a bite.)

Taig: Give me a divide of it.

Darby: Give me a drop of your own porter so, is in the bottle. There need be no dread on you now, of you being no match for your grand man.

Taig: That is so. *(Drinks.)* I'll strive no more to fit myself for high quality relations. I am free from patterns of high up cousins from this out. I'll be a pattern to myself.

Darby: I am well content being free of you, the way you were pictured to be. I declare to my goodness, the name of you put terror on me through the whole of my lifetime, and your image to be clogging and checking me on every side.

Taig: To be thinking of you being in the world was a holy terror to myself. I give you my word you came through my sleep the same as a scarecrow or a dragon.

Darby: It is great things I will be doing from this out, we two having nothing to cast up against one another. To be quit of Timothy the bogie and to get Taig for a comrade, I'm as proud as the Crown of France!

Taig: I'm in dread of neither bumble or bagman or bugaboo! I will regulate things from myself from this out.

Darby: There to be fineness of living in the world, why wouldn't I make it out for myself?

Taig: It is to the harbours of America we will work our way across the wideness of the sea. It is well able we should be to go mounting up aloft in ropes. Come on Darby out of this!

Darby: There is magic and mastery come into me! This day has put wings to my heart!

Taig: Be easy now. We are maybe not clear of the chimneys yet.

Darby: What signifies chimneys? We'll go up in them till we'll take a view of the Seven Stars! It is out beyond the hills of Burren I will cast my eye, till I'll see the three gates of Heaven!

Taig: It's like enough, luck will flow to you. The way most people fail is in not keeping up the heart. Faith, it's well you have myself to mind you. Gather up now your brush and your bag.

(They go to the door holding each other's hands and singing: "All in my hat I will cock a blue feather," etc.)

Curtain

THE FULL MOON

TO ALL SANE PEOPLE IN OR OUT OF CLOON WHO KNOW THEIR NEIGHBOURS TO BE NATURALLY CRACKED OR SOMEWAY QUEER OR TO HAVE GONE WRONG IN THE HEAD.

PERSONS [Sidenote: ALL SANE] *Shawn Early Bartley Fallon Peter Tannian Hyacinth Halvey Mrs. Broderick Miss Joyce Cracked Mary Davideen,* HER BROTHER, AN INNOCENT

THE FULL MOON

Scene: A shed close to Cloon Station; Bartley Fallon is sitting gloomily on a box; Hyacinth Halvey and Shawn Early are coming in at door.

Shawn Early: It is likely the train will not be up to its time, and cattle being on it for the fair. It's best wait in the shed. Is that Bartley Fallon? What way are you, Bartley?

Bartley Fallon: Faith, no way at all. On the drag, on the drag; striving to put the bad times over me.

Shawn Early: Is it business with the nine o'clock you have?

Bartley Fallon: The wife that is gone visiting to Tubber, and that has the door locked till such time as she will come back on the train. And I thought this shed a place where no bad thing would be apt to happen me, and not to be going through the streets, and the darkness falling.

Shawn Early: It is not long till the full moon will be rising.

Bartley Fallon: Everything that is bad, the falling sickness—God save the mark—or the like, should be at its worst at the full moon. I suppose because it is the leader of the stars.

Shawn Early: Ah, what could happen any person in the street of Cloon?

Bartley Fallon: There might. Look at Matt Finn, the coffin-maker, put his hand on a cage the circus brought, and the lion took and tore it till they stuck him with a fork you'd rise dung with, and at that he let it drop. And that was a man had never quitted Cloon.

Shawn Early: I thought you might be sending something to the fair.

Bartley Fallon: It isn't to the train I would be trusting anything I would have to sell, where it might be thrown off the track. And where would be the use sending the couple of little lambs I have? It is likely there is no one would ask me where was I going. When the weight is not in them, they won't carry the price. Sure, the grass I have is no good, but seven times worse than the road.

Shawn Early: They are saying there'll be good demand at the fair of Carrow to-morrow.

Hyacinth Halvey: To-morrow the fair day of Carrow? I was not remembering that.

Bartley Fallon: Ah, there won't be many in it, I'm thinking. There isn't a hungrier village in Connacht, they were telling me, and it's poor the look of it as well.

Hyacinth Halvey: To-morrow the fair day. There will be all sorts in the streets to-night.

Bartley Fallon: The sort that will be in it will be a bad sort—sievemakers and tramps and neuks.

Hyacinth Halvey: The tents on the fair green; there will be music in it; there was a fiddler having no legs would set men of threescore years and of fourscore years dancing. I can nearly hear his tune.

(He whistles "The Heather Broom.")

Bartley Fallon: You are apt to be going there on the train, I suppose? It is well to be you, Mr. Halvey, having a good place in the town, and the price of your fare, and maybe six times the price of it, in your pocket.

Hyacinth Halvey: I didn't think of that. I wonder could I go—for one night only—and see what the lads are doing.

Shawn Early: Are you forgetting, Mr. Halvey, that you are to meet his Reverence on the platform that is coming home from drinking water at the Spa?

Hyacinth Halvey: So I can meet him, and get in the train after him getting out.

(Mrs. Broderick and Peter Tannian come in.)

Mrs. Broderick: Is that Mr. Halvey is in it? I was looking for you at the chapel as I passed, and the Angelus bell after ringing.

Hyacinth Halvey: Business I have here, ma'am. I was in dread I might not be here before the train.

Mrs. Broderick: So you might not, indeed. That nine o'clock train you can never trust it to be late.

Hyacinth Halvey: To meet Father Gregan I am come, and maybe to go on myself.

Mrs. Broderick: Sure, I knew well you would be in haste to be before Father Gregan, and we knowing what we know.

Hyacinth Halvey: I have no business only to be showing respect to him.

Shawn Early: His good word he will give to Mr. Halvey at the Board, where it is likely he will be made Clerk of the Union next week.

Mrs. Broderick: His good word he will give to another thing besides that, I am thinking.

Hyacinth Halvey: I don't know what you are talking about.

Mrs. Broderick: Didn't you hear the news, Peter Tannian, that Mr. Halvey is apt to be linked and joined in marriage with Miss Joyce, the priest's housekeeper?

Peter Tannian: I to believe all the lies I'd hear, I'd be a racked man by this.

Mrs. Broderick: What I say now is as true as if you were on the other side of me. I suppose now the priest is come home there'll be no delay getting the license.

Hyacinth Halvey: It is not so settled as that.

Mrs. Broderick: Why wouldn't it be settled and it being told at Mrs. Delane's and through the whole world?

Peter Tannian: She should be a steady wife for him—a fortied girl.

Shawn Early: A very good fortune in the bank they are saying she has, and she having crossed the ocean twice to America.

Hartley Fallen: It's as good for him to have a woman will keep the door open before him and his victuals ready and a quiet tongue in her head. Not like that little Tartar of my own.

Mrs. Broderick. And an educated woman along with that. A man of his sort, going to be Clerk of the Union and to be taken up with books and papers, it's likely he'd die in a week, he to marry a dunce.

Bartley Fallon: So it's likely he would.

Mrs. Broderick: A little shop they are saying she will take, for to open a flour store, and you to be keeping the accounts, the way you would not spend any waste time.

Hyacinth Halvey: I have no mind to be settling myself down yet a while. I might maybe take a ramble here or there. There's many of my comrades in the States.

Mrs. Broderick: To go away from Cloon, is it? And why would you think to do that, and the whole town the same as a father and mother to you? Sure, the sergeant would live and die with you, and there are no two from this to Galway as great as yourself and the priest. To see you coming up the street, and your Dublin top-coat around you, there are some would give you a salute the same nearly as the Bishop.

Peter Tannian: They wouldn't do that maybe and they hearing things as I heard them.

Hyacinth Halvey: What things?

Peter Tannian: There was a herd passing through from Carrow. It is what I heard him saying———

Mrs. Broderick: You heard nothing of Mr. Halvey, but what is worthy of him. But that's the way always. The most thing a man does, the less he will get for it after.

Peter Tannian: A grand place in Carrow I suppose you had?

Hyacinth Halvey: I had plenty of places. Giving out proclamations—attending waterworks——.

Mrs. Broderick: It is well fitted for any place he is, and all that was written around him and he coming into Cloon.

Peter Tannian: Writing is easy.

Mrs. Broderick: Look at him since he was here, this twelvemonth back, that he never went into a dance-house or stood at a cross-road, and never lost a half-an-hour with drink. Made no blunder, made no rumours. Whatever could be said of his worth, it could not be too well said.

Hyacinth Halvey: Do you think now, ma'am, would it be any harm I to go spend a day or maybe two days out of this—I to go on the train——.

Miss Joyce: (At door, coming in backwards.) Go back now, go back! Don't be following after me in through the door! Is Mr. Halvey there? Don't let her come following me, Mr. Halvey!

Hyacinth Halvey: Who is it is in it?

(Sound of discordant singing outside.)

Miss Joyce: Cracked Mary it is, that is after coming back this day from the asylum.

Hyacinth Halvey: I never saw her, I think.

Shawn Early: The creature, she was light this long while and not good in the head, and at the last lunacy came on her and she was tied and bound. Sometimes singing and dancing she does be, and sometimes troublesome.

Miss Joyce: They had a right to keep her spancelled in the asylum. She would begrudge any respectable person to be walking the street. She'd hoot you, she'd shout you, she'd clap her hands at you. She is a blight in the town.

Hyacinth Halvey: There is a lad along with her.

Shawn Early: It is Davideen, her brother, that is innocent. He was left rambling from place to place the time she was put within walls.

(Cracked Mary and Davideen come in. Miss Joyce clings to Hyacinth's arm.)

Cracked Mary: Give me a charity now, the way I'll be keeping a little rag on me and a little shoe to my foot. Give me the price of tobacco and the price of a grain of tea; for tobacco is blessed and tea is good for the head.

Shawn Early: Give out now, Davideen, a verse of "The Heather Broom." That's a splendid tune.

Davideen: (Sings.)

Oh, don't you remember,
As it's often I told you,
As you passed through our kitchen,
That a new broom sweejps clean?
Come out now and buy one,
Come out now and try one—

(His voice cracks, and he breaks off, laughing foolishly.)

Mrs. Broderick: He has a sweet note in his voice, but to know or to understand what he is doing, he couldn't do it.

Cracked Mary: Leave him a while. His song that does be clogged through the daytime, the same as the sight is clogged with myself. It isn't but in the night time I can see anything worth while. Davy is a proper boy, a proper boy; let you leave Davy alone. It was himself came before me ere yesterday in the morning, and I walking out the madhouse door.

Shawn Early: It is often there will fiddlers be waiting to play for them coming out, that are maybe the finest dancers of the day.

Cracked Mary: Waiting before me he was, and no one to give him knowledge unless it might be the Big Man. I give you my word he near ate the face off me. As glad to see me he was as if I had dropped from heaven. Come hither to me, Davy, and give no heed to them. It is as dull and as lagging as themselves you would be maybe, and the world to be different and the moon to change its courses with the sun.

Bartley Fallon: I never would wish to be put within a madhouse before I'd die.

Cracked Mary: Sorry they were losing me. There was not a better prisoner in it than my own four bones.

Bartley Fallon: Squeals you would hear from it, they were telling me, like you'd hear at the ringing of the pigs. Savages with whips beating them the same as hounds. You would not stand and listen to them for a hundred sovereigns. Of all bad things that can come upon a man, it is certain the madness is the last.

Miss Joyce: It is likely she was well content in it, and the friends she had being of her own class.

Cracked Mary: What way could you make friends with people would be always talking? Too much of talk and of noise there was in it, cursing, and praying, and tormenting; some dancing, some singing, and one writing a letter to a she devil called Lucifer. I not to close my ears, I would have lost the sound of Davideen's song.

Miss Joyce: It was good shelter you got in it through the bad weather, and not to be out perishing under cold, the same as the starlings in the snow.

Cracked Mary: I was my seven months in it, my seven months and a day. My good clothes that went astray on me and my boots. My fine gaudy dress was all moth-eated, that was worked with the wings of birds. To fall into dust and ashes it did, and the wings rose up into the high air.

Bartley Fallen. Take care would the madness catch on to ourselves the same as the chin-cough or the pock.

Mrs. Broderick: Ah, that's not the way it goes travelling from one to another, but some that are naturally cracked and inherit it.

Shawn Early: It is a family failing with her tribe. The most of them get giddy in their latter end.

Miss Joyce: It might be it was sent as a punishment before birth, for to show the power of God.

Peter Tannian: It is tea-drinking does it, and that is the reason it is on the wife it is apt to fall for the most part.

Mrs. Broderick: Ah, there's some does be thinking their wives isn't right, and there's others think they are too right. There to be any fear of me going astray, I give you my word I'd lose my wits on the moment.

Hyacinth Halvey: There are some say it is the moon.

Shawn Early: So it is too. The time the moon is going back, the blood that is in a person does be weakening, but when the moon is strong, the blood that moves strong in the same way. And it to be at the full, it drags the wits along with it, the same as it drags the tide.

Mrs. Broderick: Those that are light show off more and have the talk of twenty the time it is at the full, that is sure enough. And to hold up a silk handkerchief and to look through it, you would see the four quarters of the moon; I was often told that.

Miss Joyce: It is not you, Mr. Halvey, will give in to an unruly thing like the moon, that is under no authority, and cannot be put back, the same as a fast day that would chance to fall upon a feast.

Hyacinth Halvey: It is likely it is put in the sky the same as a clock for our use, the way you would pick knowledge of the weather, the time the stars would be wild about it.

Mrs. Broderick: That is very nice now. The thing you'd know, you'd like to go on, and to hear more or less about it.

Miss Joyce: (To H.H.) It is a lantern for your own use it will be to-night, and his Reverence coming home through the street, and yourself coming along with him to the house.

Mrs. Broderick: That's right, Miss Joyce. Keep a good grip of him. What do you say to him talking a while ago as if his mind was running on some thought to leave Cloon?

Miss Joyce: What way could he leave it?

Hyacinth Halvey: No way at all, I'm thinking, unless there would be a miracle worked by the moon.

Mrs. Broderick: Ah, miracles is gone out of the world this long time, with education, unless that they might happen in your own inside.

Miss Joyce: I'll go set the table and kindle the fire, and I'll come back to meet the train with you myself.

(She goes. A noise heard outside.)

Hyacinth Halvey: What is that now?

Shawn Early: (At door.) Some noise as of running.

Hartley Fallon: (Going to door.) It might chance to be some prisoner they would be bringing to the train.

Peter Tannian: No, but some lads that are running.

(They go out. H.H. is going too, but Mrs. Broderick goes before him and turns him round in doorway.)

Mrs. Broderick: Don't be coming out now in the dust that was formed by the heat is in the breeze. It would be a pity to spoil your Dublin coat, or your shirt that is that white you would nearly take it to be blue.

(She goes out, pushing him in and shutting door after her.)

Cracked Mary: Ha! ha! ha!

Hyacinth Halvey: What is it you are laughing at?

Cracked Mary: Ha! ha! ha! It is a very laughable thing now, the third most laughable thing I ever met with in my lifetime.

Hyacinth Halvey: What is that?

Cracked Mary: A fine young man to be shut up and bound in a narrow little shed, and the full moon rising, and I knowing what I know!

Hyacinth Halvey: It's little you are likely to know about me.

Cracked Mary: Tambourines and fiddles and pipes—melodeons and the whistling of drums.

Hyacinth Halvey: I suppose it is the Carrow fair you are talking about.

Cracked Mary: Sitting within walls, and a top-coat wrapped around him, and mirth and music and frolic being in the place we know, and some dancing sets on the floor.

Hyacinth Halvey: I wish I wasn't in this place tonight. I would like well to be going on the train, if it wasn't for the talk the neighbours would be making. I would like well to slip away. It is a long time I am going without any sort of funny comrades.

(Goes to door. The others enter quickly, pushing him back.)

Bartley Fallon: Nothing at all to see. It would be best for us to have stopped where we were.

Mrs. Broderick: Running like foals to see it, and nothing to be in it worth while.

Hyacinth Halvey: What was it was in it?

Shawn Early: Nothing at all but some lads that were running in pursuit of a dog.

Bartley Fallon: Near knocked us they did, and they coming round the corner of the wall.

Hyacinth Halvey: Is it that it was a mad dog?

Peter Tannian: Ah, what mad? Mad dogs are done away with now by the head Government and muzzles and the police.

Bartley Fallon: They are more watchful over them than they used. But all the same, you to see a strange dog afar off, you would be uneasy, thinking it might be yourself he would be searching out as his prey.

Mrs. Broderick: Sure, there did a dog go mad through Galway, and the whole town rose against him, and flocked him into a corner, and shot him there. He did no harm after, he being made an end of at the first.

Shawn Early: It might be that dog they were pursuing after was mad, on the head of being under the full moon.

Cracked Mary: (Jumping up excitedly.) That mad dog, he is a Dublin dog; he is betune you and Belfast—he is running ahead—you couldn't keep up with him.

Hyacinth Halvey: There is one, so, mad upon the road.

Cracked Mary: There is police after him, but they cannot come up with him; he destroyed a splendid sow; nine bonavs they buried or less.

Shawn Early: What place is he gone now?

Cracked Mary: He made off towards Craughwell, and he bit a fine young man.

Bartley Fallen: So he would too. Sure, when a mad dog would be going about, on horseback or wherever you are, you're ruined.

Cracked Mary: That dog is going on all the time; he wouldn't stop, but go ahead and bring that mouthful with him. He is still on the road; he is keeping the middle of the road; they say he is as big as a calf.

Hyacinth Halvey: It is the police I have a right to forewarn to go after him.

Cracked Mary: The motor cars is going to get out to track him, for fear he would destroy the world!

Mrs. Broderick: That is a very nice thought now, to be sending the motor cars after him to overturn and to crush him the same as an ass-car in their path.

Cracked Mary: You can't save yourself from a dog; he is after his own equals, dogs. He is doing every harm. They are out night and day.

Shawn Early: Sure, a mad dog would go from this to Kinvara in a half a minute, like the train.

Cracked Mary: He won't stay in this country down—he goes the straight road—he takes by the wind. He is as big as a yearling calf.

Mrs. Broderick: I wouldn't ever forgive myself I to see him.

Cracked Mary: He is not very heavy yet. There is only the relics in him.

Hyacinth Halvey: They have a right to bring their rifles in their hand.

Cracked Mary: The police is afraid of their life. They wrote for motor cars to follow him. Sure, he'd destroy the beasts of the field. A milch cow, he to grab at her, she's settled. Terrible wicked he is; he's as big as five dogs, and he does be very strong. I hope in the Lord he'll be caught. It will be a blessing from the Almighty God to kill that dog.

Hyacinth Halvey: He is surely the one is raging through the street.

Peter Tannian: Why wouldn't he be him? Is it likely there would be two of them in it at the one time?

Shawn Early: A queer cut of a dog he was; a lurcher, a bastard hound.

Peter Tannian: I would say him to be about the size of the foal of a horse.

Mrs. Broderick: Didn't he behave well not to do ourselves an injury?

Bartley Fallon: It is likely he will do great destruction. I wouldn't say but I felt the weight of him and his two paws around my neck.

Hyacinth Halvey: I will go out following him.

Shawn Early: (Holding him). Oh, let you not endanger yourself! It is the peelers should go follow him, that are armed with their batons and their guns.

Hyacinth Halvey: I'll go. He might do some injury going through the town.

Mrs. Broderick: Ah now, it is not yourself we would let go into danger! It is Peter Tannian should go, if any person should go.

Peter Tannian: Is it Hyacinth Halvey you are taking to be so far before myself?

Mrs. Broderick: Why wouldn't he be before you?

Peter Tannian: Ask him what was he in Carrow? Ask was he a sort of a corner-boy, ringing the bell, pumping water, gathering a few coppers in the daytime for to scatter on a game of cards.

Hyacinth Halvey: Stop your lies and your chat!

Mrs. Broderick: (to Tannian) You are going light in the head to talk that way.

Shawn Early: He is, and queer in the mind. Take care did he get a bite from the dog, that left some venom working in his blood.

Hyacinth Halvey: So he might, and he having a sort of a little rent in his sleeve.

Peter Tannian: I to have got a bite from the dog, is it? I did not come anear him at all. You to strip me as bare as winter you will not find the track of his teeth. It is Shawn Early was nearer to him than what I was.

Shawn Early: I was not nearer, or as near as what Mrs. Broderick was.

Mrs. Broderick: I made away when I saw him. My chest is not the better of it yet. Since I left off fretting I got gross. I am that nervous I would run from a blessed sheep, let alone a dog.

Shawn Early: To see any of the signs of madness upon him, it is Mr. Halvey the sergeant would look to for to make his report.

Hyacinth Halvey: So I would make a report.

Peter Tannian: Is it that you lay down you can see signs? Is that the learning they were giving you in Carrow?

Mrs. Broderick: Don't be speaking with him at all. It is easy know the signs. A person to be laughing and mocking, and that would not have the same habits with yourself, or to have no fear of things you would be in dread of, or to be using a different class of food.

Peter Tannian: I use no food but clean food.

Hyacinth Halvey: To be giddy in the head is a sign, and to be talking of things that passed years ago.

Peter Tannian: I am talking of nothing but the thing I have a right to talk of.

Mrs. Broderick: To be nervous and thinking and pausing, and playing with knicknacks.

Peter Tannian: It never was my habit to be playing with knicknacks.

Bartley Fallon: When the master in the school where I was went queer, he beat me with two clean rods, and wrote my name with my own blood.

Mrs. Broderick: To take the shoe off their foot, and to hit out right and left with it, bawling their life out, tearing their clothes, scattering and casting them in every part; or to run naked through the town, and all the people after them.

Shawn Early: To be jumping the height of trees they do be, and all the people striving to slacken them.

Hyacinth Halvey: To steal prayer-books and rosaries, and to be saying prayers they never could keep in mind before.

Mrs. Broderick: Very strong, that they could leap a wall—jumping and pushing and kicking—or to tie people to one another with a rope.

Shawn Early: Any fear of any person here being violent, Mr. Halvey will get him put under restraint.

Peter Tannian: Is it myself you are thinking to put under restraint? Would a man would be pushing and kicking and tearing his clothes, be able to do arithmetic on a board? Look now at that. *(Chalks figures on door.)* Three and three makes six!—and three—

Mrs. Broderick: I'm no hand at figuring, but I can say out a blessed hymn, what any person with the mind gone contrary in them could not do. Hearken now till you'll know is there confusion in my mind. *(Sings.)*

Mary Broderick is my name;
Fiddane was my station;
Cloon is my dwelling-place;
And (I hope) heaven is my destination.

Mary Broderick is my name,
Cloon was my—

Cracked Mary: (With a cackle of delight.) Give heed to them now, Davideen! That's the way the crazed people used to be going on in the place where I was, every one thinking the other to be cracked.

Hyacinth Halvey: (To Tannian.) Look now at your great figuring! Argus with his hundred eyes wouldn't know is that a nought or is it a nine without a tail.

Peter Tannian: Leave that blame on a little ridge that is in the nature of the chalk. Look now at Mary Broderick, that it has failed to word out her verse.

Mrs. Broderick: Ah, what signifies? I'd never get light greatly. It wouldn't be worth while I to go mad.

(Bartley Fallon gives a deep groan.)

Shawn Early: What is on you, Bartley?

Bartley Fallon: I'm in dread it is I myself has got the venom into my blood.

Hyacinth Halvey: What makes you think that?

Bartley Fallon: It's a sort of a thing would be apt to happen me, and any malice to fall within the town at all.

Mrs. Broderick: Give heed to him, Hyacinth Halvey; you are the most man we have to baffle any wrong thing coming in our midst!

Hyacinth Halvey: Is it that you are feeling any pain as of a wound or a sore?

Bartley Fallon: Some sort of a little catch I'm thinking there is in under my knee. I would feel no pain unless I would turn it contrary.

Hyacinth Halvey: What class of feeling would you say you are feeling?

Bartley Fallon: I am feeling as if the five fingers of my hand to be lessening from me, the same as five farthing dips the heat of the sun would be sweating the tallow from.

Hyacinth Halvey: That is a strange account.

Bartley Fallon: And a sort of a megrim in my head, the same as a sheep would get a fit of staggers in a field.

Hyacinth Halvey: That is what I would look for. Is there some sort of a roaring in your ear?

Bartley Fallon: There is, there is, as if I would hear voices would be talking.

Hyacinth Halvey: Would you feel any wish to go tearing and destroying?

Bartley Fallon: I would indeed, and there to be an enemy upon my path. Would you say now, Widow Broderick, am I getting anyway flushy in the face?

Mrs. Broderick: Don't leave your eye off him for pity's sake. He is reddening as red as a rose.

Bartley Fallon: I could as if walk on the wind with lightness. Something that is rising in my veins the same as froth would be rising on a pint.

Hyacinth Halvey: It is the doctor I'd best call for—and maybe the sergeant and the priest.

Bartley Fallon: There are three thoughts going through my mind—to hang myself or to drown myself, or to cut my neck with a reaping-hook.

Mrs. Broderick: It is the doctor will serve him best, where it is the mad blood that should be bled away. To break up eggs, the white of them, in a tin can, will put new blood in him, and whiskey, and to taste no food through twenty-one days.

Bartley Fallon: I'm thinking so long a fast wouldn't serve me. I wouldn't wish the lads will bear my body to the grave, to lay down there was nothing within it but a grasshopper or a wisp of dry grass.

Shawn Early: No, but to cut a piece out of his leg the doctor will, the way the poison will get no leave to work.

Peter Tannian: Or to burn it with red-hot irons, the way it will not scatter itself and grow. There does a doctor do that out in foreign.

Mrs. Broderick: It would be more natural to cut the leg off him in some sort of a Christian way.

Shawn Early: If it was a pig was bit, or a sow or a bonav, it to show the signs, it would be shot, if it was a whole fleet of them was in it.

Mrs. Broderick: I knew of a man that was butler in a big house was bit, and they tied him first and smothered him after, and his master shot the dog. A splendid shot he was; the thing he'd not see he'd hit it the same as the thing he'd see. I heard that from an outside neighbour of my own, a woman that told no lies.

Shawn Early: Sure, they did the same thing to a high-up lady over in England, and she after being bit by her own little spaniel and it having a ring around its neck.

Peter Tannian: That is the only best thing to do. Whether the bite is from a dog, or a cat, or whatever it may be, to put the quilt and the blankets on the person and smother him in the bed. To smother them out-and-out you should, before the madness will work.

Hyacinth Halvey: I'd be loth he to be shot or smothered. I'd sooner to give him a chance in the asylum.

Mrs. Broderick: To keep him there and to try him through three changes of the moon. It's well for you, Bartley, Mr. Halvey being in charge of you, that is known to be a tender man.

Peter Tannian: He to have got a bite and to go biting others, he would put in them the same malice. It is the old people used to tell that down, and they must have had some reason doing that.

Shawn Early: To get a bite of a dog you must chance your life. There is no doubt at all about that. It might work till the time of the new moon or the full moon, and then they must be shot or smothered.

Hyacinth Halvey: It is a pity there to be no cure found for it in the world.

Shawn Early: There never came out from the Almighty any cure for a mad dog.

(Bartley Fallon has been edging towards door.)

Shawn Early: Oh! stop him and keep a hold of him, Mr. Halvey!

Hyacinth Halvey: Stop where you are.

Bartley Fallon: Isn't it enough to have madness before me, that you will not let me go fall in my own choice place?

Hyacinth Halvey: The neighbours would think it bad of me to let a raving man out into their midst.

Bartley Fallon: Is it to shoot me you are going?

Hyacinth Halvey: I will call to the doctor to say is the padded room at the workhouse the most place where you will be safe, till such time as it will be known did the poison wear away.

Bartley Fallon: I will not go in it! It is likely I might be forgot in it, or the nurses to be in dread to bring me nourishment, and they to hear me barking within the door. I'm thinking it was allotted by nature I never would die an easy death.

Hyacinth Halvey: I will keep a watch over you myself.

Bartley Fallon: Where's the use of that the time the breath will be gone out of me, and you maybe playing cards on my coffin, and I having nothing around or about me but the shroud, and the habit, and the little board?

Hyacinth Halvey: Sure, I cannot leave you the way you are.

Bartley Fallon: It is what I ever and always heard, a dog to bite you, all you have to do is to take a pinch of its hair and to lay it into the wound.

Mrs. Broderick: So I heard that myself. A dog to bite any person he is entitled to be plucked of his hair.

Hyacinth Halvey: I'll go out; I might chance to see him.

Mrs. Broderick: You will not, without getting advice from the priest that is coming in the train. Let his Reverence come into this place, and say is it Bartley or is it Peter Tannian was done destruction on by the dog.

Shawn Early: There is a surer way than that.

Mrs. Broderick: What way?

Shawn Early: It takes madness to find out madness. Let you call to the cracked woman that should know.

Hyacinth Halvey: Come hither, Mary, and tell us is there any one of your own sort in this shed?

Mrs. Broderick: That is a good thought. It is only themselves that recognise one another.

Bartley Fallon: Do not ask her! I will not leave it to her!

Mrs. Broderick: Sure, she cannot say more than what yourself has said against yourself.

Bartley Fallon: I'm in dread she might know too much, and be telling out what is within in my mind.

Hyacinth Halvey: That's foolishness. These are not the ancient times, when Ireland was full of haunted people.

Bartley Fallon: Is a man having a wife and three acres of land to be put under the judgment of a witch?

Hyacinth Halvey: I would not give in to any pagan thing, but to recognise one of her own sort, that is a thing can be understood.

Mrs. Broderick: So it could be too, the same as witnesses in a court.

Bartley Fallon: I will not give in to going to demons or druids or freemasons! Wasn't there enough of misfortune set before my path through every day of my lifetime without it to be linked with me after my death? Is it that you would force me to lose the comforts of heaven and to get the poverty of hell? I tell you I will have no trade with witches! I would sooner go face the featherbeds.

Hyacinth Halvey: Say out, girl, do you see any craziness here or anything of the sort?

Cracked Mary: Every day in the year there comes some malice into the world, and where it comes from is no good place.

Mrs. Broderick: That is it, a venomous dew, as in the year of the famine. There is no astronomer can say it is from the earth or the sky.

Hyacinth Halvey: It is what we are asking you, did any of that malice get its scope in this place?

Cracked Mary: That was settled in Mayo two thousand years ago.

Mrs. Broderick: Ah, there's no head or tail to that one's story. You 'd be left at the latter end the same as at the commencement.

Hyacinth Halvey: That dog you were talking of, that is raging through the district and the town—did it leave any madness after it?

Cracked Mary: It will go in the wind, there is a certain time for that. It might go off in the wind again. It might go shaping off and do no harm.

Bartley Fallon: Where is that dog presently, till some person might go pluck out a few ribs of its hair?

Cracked Mary: Raging ever and always it is, raging wild. Sure, that is a dog was in it before the foundations of the world.

Peter Tannian: Who is it now that venom fell on, whatever beast's jaws may have scattered it?

Cracked Mary: It is the full moon knows that. The moon to slacken it is safe, there is no harm in it. Almighty God will do that much. He'll slacken it like you 'd slacken lime.

Shawn Early: There is reason in what she is saying. Set open the door and let the full moon call its own!

Bartley Fallon: Don't let in the rays of it upon us or I'm a gone man. It to shine on them that are going wrong in the head, it would raise a great stir in the mind. Sure, it's in the asylum at that time they do have whips to chastise them.

(Goes to corner.)

Cracked Mary: That's it. The moon is terrible. The full moon cracks them out and out, any one that would have any spleen or any relics in them.

Mrs. Broderick: Do not let in the light of it. I would scruple to look at it myself.

Cracked Mary: Let you throw open the door, Davideen. It is not ourselves are in dread that the white man in the sky will be calling names after us and ridiculing us. Ha! ha! I might be as foolish as yourselves and as fearful, but for the Almighty that left a little cleft in my skull, that would let in His candle through the night time.

Hyacinth Halvey: Hurry on now, tell us is there any one in this place is wild and astray like yourself.

(He opens the door. The light falls on him.)

Cracked Mary: (Putting her hand on him.) There was great shouting in the big round house, and you coming into it last night.

Hyacinth Halvey: What are you saying? I never went frolicking in the night time since the day I came into Cloon.

Cracked Mary: We were talking of it a while ago. I knew you by the smile and by the laugh of you. A queen having a yellow dress, and the hair on her smooth like marble. All the dead of the village were in it, and of the living myself and yourself.

Hyacinth Halvey: I thought it was of Carrow she was talking; it is of the other world she is raving, and of the shadow-shapes of the forth.

Cracked Mary: You have the door open—the speckled horses are on the road!—make a leap on the horse as it goes by, the horse that is without a rider. Can't you hear them puffing and roaring? Their breath is like a fog upon the air.

Hyacinth Halvey: What you hear is but the train puffing afar off.

Cracked Mary: Make a snap at the bridle as it passes by the bush in the western gap. Run out now, run, where you have the bare ridge of the world before you, and no one to take orders from but yourself, maybe, and God.

Hyacinth Halvey: Ah, what way can I run to any place!

Cracked Mary: Stop where you are, so. In my opinion it is little difference the moon can see between the whole of ye. Come on, Davideen, come out now, we have the wideness of the night before us. O golden God! All bad things quieten in the night time, and the ugly thing itself will put on some sort of a decent face! Come out now to the night that will give you the song, and will show myself out as beautiful as Helen of the Greek gods, that hanged herself the day there first came a wrinkle on her face!

Davideen: (Coming close, and taking her hand as he sings.)

Oh! don't you remember
What our comrades called to us
And they footing steps
At the call of the moon?
Come out to the rushes,
Come out to the bushes,
Where the music is called
By the lads of Queen Anne!

(They look beautiful. They dance and sing in perfect time as they go out.)

Peter Tannian: (Closing the door, and pointing at Hyacinth, who stands gazing after them, and when the door is shut sits down thinking deeply.) It is on him her judgment fell, and a clear judgment.

Shawn Early: She gave out that award fair enough.

Peter Tannian: Did you take notice, and he coming into the shed, he had like some sort of a little twist in his walk?

Mrs. Broderick: I would be loth to think there would be any poison lurking in his veins. Where now would it come from, and Cracked Mary's dog being as good as no dog at all?

Peter Tannian: It might chance, and he a child in the cradle, to get the bite of a dog. It might be only now, its full time being come, its power would begin to work.

Mrs. Broderick: So it would too, and he but to see the shadow of the dog bit him in a body glass, or in the waves, and he himself looking over a boat, and as if called to throw himself in the tide. But I would not have thought it of Mr. Halvey. Well, it's as hard to know what might be spreading abroad in any person's mind, as to put the body of a horse out through a cambric needle.

(Hyacinth looks at them.)

Shawn Early: Be quiet now, he is going to say some word.

Hyacinth Halvey: There is a thought in my mind. I think it was coming this good while.

Shawn Early: Whisht now and listen.

Hyacinth Halvey: I made a great mistake coming into this place.

Peter Tannian: There was some mistake made anyway.

Hyacinth: It is foolishness kept me in it ever since. It is too big a name was put upon me.

Peter Tannian: It is the power of the moon is forcing the truth out of him.

Hyacinth Halvey: Every person in the town giving me out for more than I am. I got too much of that in the heel.

Shawn Early: He is talking queer now anyway.

Hyacinth Halvey: Calling to me every little minute—expecting me to do this thing and that thing—watching me the same as a watchdog, their eyes as if fixed upon my face.

Mrs. Broderick: To be giving out such strange thoughts, he hasn't much brains left around him.

Hyacinth Halvey: I looking to be Clerk of the Union, and the place I had giving me enough to do, and too much to do. Tied on this side, tied on that side. I to be bothered with business through the holy livelong day!

Peter Tannian: It is good pay he got with it. Eighty pounds a year doesn't come on the wind.

Hyacinth Halvey: In danger to be linked and wed—I never ambitioned it—with a woman would want me to be earning through every day of the year.

Shawn Early: He is a gone man surely.

Hyacinth Hakey: The wide ridge of the world before me, and to have no one to look to for orders; that would be better than roast and boiled and all the comforts of the day. I declare to goodness, and I 'd nearly take my oath, I 'd sooner be among a fleet of tinkers, than attending meetings of the Board!

Mrs. Broderick: If there are fairies in it, it is in the fairies he is.

Peter Tannian: Give me a hold of that chain.

Mrs. Broderick: What is it you are about to do?

Peter Tannian: To bind him to the chair I will before he will burst out wild mad. Come over here, Bartley Fallon, and lend a hand if you can.

(Bartley Fallon appears from corner with a chicken crate over his head.)

Mrs. Broderick: O Bartley, that is the strangest lightness ever I saw, to go bind a chicken crate around your skull!

Bartley Fallon: Will you tighten the knots I have tied, Peter Tannian! I am in dread they might slacken or fail.

Shawn Early: Was there ever seen before this night such power to be in the moon!

Bartley Fallon: It would seem to be putting very wild unruly thoughts a-through me, stirring up whatever spleen or whatever relics was left in me by the nature of the dog.

Peter Tannian: Is it that you think those rods, spaced wide, as they are, will keep out the moon from entering your brain?

Bartley Fallon: There does great strength come at the time the wits would be driven out of a person. I never was handled by a policeman—but once—and never hit a blow on any man. I would not wish to destroy my neighbour or to have his blood on my hands.

Shawn Early: It is best keep out of his reach.

Bartley Fallon: The way I have this fixed, there is no person will be the worse for me. I to rush down the street and to meet with my most enemy in some lonesome craggy place, it would fail me, and I thrusting for it to scatter any share of poison in his body or to sink my teeth in his skin. I wouldn't wonder I to have hung for some of you, and that plan not to have come into my head.

(Whistle of train heard.)

Hyacinth Halvey: (Getting up.) I have my mind made up, I am going out of this on that train.

Peter Tannian: You are not going so easy as what you think.

Hyacinth Halvey: Let you mind your own business.

Peter Tannian: I am well able to mind it.

Hyacinth Halvey: (Throwing off top-coat.) You cannot keep me here.

Peter Tannian: Give me a hand with the chain. *(They throw it round Hyacinth and hold him.)*

Hyacinth Halvey: Is it out of your senses you are gone?

Peter Tannian: Not at all, but yourself that is gone raving mad from the fury and the strength of some dog.

Miss Joyce: (At door.) Are you there, Hyacinth Halvey? The train is in. Come forward now, and give a welcome to his Reverence.

Hyacinth Halvey: Let me go out of this!

Miss Joyce: You are near late as it is. The train is about to start.

Hyacinth Halvey: Let me go, or I'll tear the heart out of ye!

Shawn Early: Oh, he is stark, staring mad!

Hyacinth Halvey: Mad, am I? Bit by a dog, am I? You'll see am I mad! I'll show madness to you! Let go your hold or I'll skin you! I'll destroy you! I'll bite you! I'm a red enemy to the whole of you! Leave go your grip! Yes, I'm mad! Bow wow wow, wow wow!

(They let go and fall back in terror, and he rushes out of the door.)

Miss Joyce: What at all has happened? Where is he gone?

Shawn Early: To the train he is gone, and away in it he is gone.

Miss Joyce: He gave some sort of a bark or a howl.

Shawn Early: He is gone clean mad. Great arguing he had, and leaping and roaring.

Bartley Fallon: (Taking off crate.) He went very near to tear us all asunder. I declare I amn't worth a match.

Mrs. Broderick: He made a reel in my head, till I don't know am I right myself.

Shawn Early: Bawling his life out, tearing his clothes, tearing and eating them. Look at his top-coat he left after him.

Bartley Fallon: He poured all over with pure white foam.

Peter Tannian: There now is an end of your elegant man.

Shawn Early: Bit he was with the mad dog that went tearing, and lads chasing him a while ago.

Miss Joyce: Sure that was Tannian's own dog, that had a bit of meat snapped from Quirke's ass-car. He is without this door now. *(All look out.)* He has the appearance of having a full meal taken.

Bartley Fallon: And they to be saying I went mad. That is the way always, and a thing to be tasked to me that was not in it at all.

Mrs. Broderick: (Laying her hand on Miss Joyce's shoulder.) Take comfort now; and if it was the moon done all, and has your bachelor swept, let you not begrudge it its full share of praise for the hand it had in banishing a strange bird, might have gone wild and bawling like eleven, and you after being wed with him, and would maybe have put a match to the roof. And hadn't you the luck of the world now, that you did not give notice to the priest!

Curtain

COATS

Hazel EDITOR OF "CHAMPION" *Mineog* EDITOR OF "TRIBUNE" *John* A WAITER

Scene: Dining room of Royal Hotel Cloonmore.

Hazel: (Coming in.) Did Mr. Mineog come yet, John?

John: He did not, Mr. Hazel. Ah, he won't be long coming. It's seldom he does be late.

Hazel: Is the dinner ready?

John: It is, sir. Boiled beef and parsnips, the same as every Monday for all comers, and an apple pie for yourself and Mr. Mineog.

Mineog: (Coming in.) Mr. Hazel is the first tonight. I'm glad to see you looking so good.

(They take off coats and give to waiter.)

Mineog: Put that on its own peg.

Hazel: And mine on its own peg to the rear.

John: I will, sir.

> *(He drops coats in putting them up. Then notices broken pane in window and picks up the coats hurriedly, putting them on wrong pegs. Hazel and Mineog have sat down.)*

Hazel: Have you any strange news?

Mineog: I have but the same news I always have, that it is quick Monday comes around, and that it is hard make provision for to fill up the four sheets of the *Tribune*, and nothing happening in these parts worth while. There would seem to be no news on this day beyond all days of the year.

Hazel: Sure there is the same care and the same burden on myself. I wish I didn't put a supplement to the *Champion*. The deer knows what way will I fill it between this and Thursday, or in what place I can go questing after news!

Mineog: Last week passed without anything doing. It is a very backward place to give information for two papers. If it was not for the league is between us, and for us meeting here on every Monday to make sure we are taking different sides on every question may turn up, and giving every abuse to one another in print, there is no person would pay his penny for the two of them, or it may be for the one of them.

Hazel: That is so. And the worst is, there is no question ever rises that we do not agree on, or that would have power to make us fall out in earnest. It was different in my early time. The questions used to rise up then were worth fighting for.

Mineog: There are some people so cantankerous they will heat themselves in argument as to which side might be right or wrong in a war, or if wars should be in it at all, or hangings.

Hazel: Ah, when they are as long on the road as we are, they'll take things easy. *Mineog:* Now all the kingdoms of the earth to go struggling on one wrong side or another, or to bring themselves down to dust and ashes, it would not break our friendship. In all the years past there never did a cross word rise between us.

Hazel: There never will. What are the fights of politics and parties beside living neighbourly with one another, and to go peaceable to the grave, our selves that are the oldest residents in the Square.

Mineog: It will be long indeed before you will be followed to the grave. You didn't live no length yet. You are too fresh to go out and to forsake your wife and your family.

Hazel: Ah, when the age would be getting up on you, you wouldn't be getting younger. But it's yourself that is as full of spirit as a four-year-old. I wish I had a sovereign for every year you will reign after me in the Square.

Mineog: (Sneezes.) There is a draught of air coming in the window.

Hazel: (Rising.) Take care might it be open—no, but a pane that is out. There is a very chilly breeze sweeping in.

Mineog: (Rising.) I will put on my coat so. There is no use giving provocation to a cold.

Hazel: I'll do the same myself. It is hard to banish a sore throat.

(They put on coats. John brings in dinner. They sit down.)

Mineog: See can you baffle that draught of air, John.

John: I'll go in search of something to stop it, sir. This bit of a board I brought is too unshapely.

Mineog: Two columns of the *Tribune* as empty yet as anything you could see. I had them kept free for the Bishop's speech and he didn't come after.

Hazel: That's the same cause has left myself with so wide a gap.

Mineog: In the years past there used always to be something happening such as famines, or the invention of printing. The whole world has got very slack.

Hazel: You are a better hand than what I am at filling odd spaces would be left bare. It is often I think the news you put out comes partly from your own brain, and the prophecies you lay down about the weather and the crops.

Mineog: Ah, I might stick in a bit of invention sometimes, when I'm put to the pin of my collar.

Hazel: I might maybe make an attack on the *Tribune* for that.

Mineog: Ah, what is it but a white sin. Sure it tells every person the same thing. It doesn't tell many lies, it goes somewhere a near it.

Hazel: I spent a good while this evening searching through the shelves of the press I have in the office. I write an article an odd time, when there is nothing doing, that might come handy in a hurry.

Mineog: So have I a press of the sort, and shelves in it. I am after going through them to-day.

Hazel: But it's hard find a thing would be suitable, unless you might dress it up again someway fresh.

Mineog: I made a thought and I searching a while ago. I was thinking it would be a very nice thing to show respect to yourself, and friendliness, putting down a short account of you and of all you have done for your family and for the town.

Hazel: That is a strange thing now! I had it in my mind to do the very same service to yourself.

Mineog: Is that so?

Hazel: Your worth and your generosity and the way you have worked the *Tribune* for your own and for the public good.

Mineog: And another thing. I not only thought to write it but I am after writing it.

Hazel: *(Suspiciously.)* You had not much time for that.

Mineog: I never was one to spare myself in anything that could benefit a friend.

Hazel: Neither would I spare myself. I have my article wrote.

Mineog: I have a mind to read my own one to you, the way you will know there is nothing in it but what is friendly and is kind.

Hazel: I will do the same thing. There's nothing I have said in it but what you will like to be hearing.

Mineog: *(Who has rummaged pockets.)* I thought I put it in the inside pocket—no matter—here it is.

Hazel: *(Rummaging.)* Here is my one. I was thinking I had it lost.

Mineog: *(Reading, after he has turned over a couple of sheets rapidly)* "Born and bred in this Square, he took his chief pride in his native town."

Hazel: (Turning over two sheets.) "It was in this parish and district he spent the most part of his promising youth—Richly stored with world-wide knowledge."

Mineog: "Well able to give out an opinion on any matter at all."

Hazel: "To lay down his mind on paper it would be hard to beat him."

Mineog: "With all that, humble that he would halt and speak to you the same as a child——" I'm maybe putting it down a bit too simple, but the printer will give it a little shaping after.

Hazel: So will my own printer be lengthening out the words for me according to the type and the letters of the alphabet he will have plentiful and to spare.

Mineog: "Well looking and well thought of. A true Irishman in supporting all forms of sport."

Hazel: What's that? I never was one for betting on races or gaining prizes for riddles.

Mineog: It is strange now I have no recollection of putting that down. It is I myself in the days gone by would put an odd shilling on a horse.

Hazel: These typewriters would bother the world. Wait now—let me throw an eye on those papers you have in your hand.

Mineog: Not at all. I would sooner be giving it out to you myself.

Hazel: Of course it is very pleasing to be listening to so nice an account—but lend it a minute.

(Puts out hand.)

Mineog: Bring me now a bottle of wine, John—you know the sort—till I'll drink to Mr. Hazel's good health.

John: I will, sir.

Hazel: No, but bring it at my own expense till I will drink to Mr. Mineog. Just give me a hold of that paper for one minute only.

Mineog: Keep patience now. I will go through it with no delay.

Hazel: (Making a snap.) Just for one minute.

Mineog: (Clapping his hand on it.) What a hurry you are in! Stop now till I'll find the place. "Very rarely indeed has been met with so fair and so neighbourly a man."

Hazel: Give me a look at it.

Mineog: What is it ails you? You are uneasy about something. What is it you are hiding from me?

Hazel: What would I have to hide but that the papers got mixed in some way, and you have in your hand what I wrote about yourself, and not what you wrote about myself?

Mineog: What way did they get into the wrong pocket now?

Hazel: (Putting MS. in his pocket.) Give me back my own and I will give you back your own.

Mineog: I don't know. You are putting it in my mind there might be something underhand. I would like to make sure what did you say about me in the heel. *(Turns over.)* "He was honest and widely respected." *Was* honest—are you saying me to be a rogue at this time?

Hazel: That's not fair dealing to be searching through it against my will.

Mineog: "He was trusted through the whole townland." *Was* trusted—is it that you are making me out to be a thief?

Hazel: Well, follow your own road and take your own way.

Mineog: "——Mr. Mineog leaves no family to lament his loss, but along with the *Tribune*, which he fostered with the care of a father, we offer up prayers for the repose of his soul." *(Stands up.)* It is a notice of my death you are after writing!

Hazel: You should understand that.

Mineog: An obituary notice! Of myself! Is it that you expect me to quit the living world between this and Thursday?

Hazel: I had no thought of the kind.

Mineog: I'm not stretched yet! What call have you to go offer prayers for me?

Hazel: I tell you I had it put by this long time till I would have occasion to use it.

Mineog: Is it this long time, so, you have been waiting for my death?

Hazel: Not at all.

Mineog: You to kill me to-day and to think to bury me to-morrow!

Hazel: Can't you listen? I was wanting something to fill space.

Mineog: Would nothing serve you to fill space but only my own corpse? To go set my coffin making and to put nettles growing on my hearth!

Wouldn't it be enough to rob my house or to make an attack upon my means? Wouldn't that fill up the gap?

Hazel: Let you not twist it that way!

Mineog: The time I was in the face of my little dinner to go startle me with a thing of the sort! I'm not worth the ground I stand on! For the *Champion* of next Thursday! I to be dead ere Thursday!

Hazel: I looked for no such thing.

Mineog: What is it makes you say me to be done and dying? Am I reduced in the face?

Hazel: You are not.

Mineog: Am I yellow and pale and shrunken?

Hazel: Why would you be?

Mineog: Would you say me to be crampy in the body? Am I staggery in the legs?

Hazel: I see no such signs.

Mineog: Is it in my hand you see them? Is it lame or is it freezed-brittle like ice?

Hazel: It is as warm and as good as my own.

Mineog: Let me take a hold of you till you will tell me has it the feel of a dead man's grip.

Hazel: I know that it has not.

Mineog: Is it shaking like a bunch of timber shavings?

Hazel: Not at all, not at all.

Mineog: It should be my hearing that is failing from me, or that I am crippled and have lost my walk.

Hazel: You are roaring and bawling without sense.

Mineog: Let the *Champion* go to flitters before I will die to please it! I will not give in to it driving me out of the world before my hour is spent! It would hardly ask that of a man would be of no use and no account, or even of a beast of any consequence.

Hazel: Who is asking you to die?

Mineog: Giving no time hardly for the priest to overtake me and to give me the rites of the Church!

Hazel: I tell you there is no danger of you giving up at all! Every person knows there must some sickness come before death. Some take it from a neighbour and it is put on others by God.

Mineog: Even so, it's hard say.

Hazel: You have not a ha'p'orth on you. No complaint in the world wide.

Mineog: That's nothing! Sickness comes upon some as sudden as to clap their hands.

Hazel: What are you talking about? You are thinking us to be in the days of the cholera yet!

Mineog: There are yet other diseases besides that.

Hazel: You put the measles over you and we going the road to school.

Mineog: There is more than measles has power bring a man down.

Hazel: You had the chin-cough passed and you rising. We were cut at the one time for the pock.

Mineog: A disease to be allotted to you it would find you out, and you maybe up twenty mile in the air!

Hazel: Ah, what disease could have you swept in the course of the next two days?

Mineog: That is what I'm after saying—unless you might have murder in your mind?

Hazel: Ah, what murder!

Mineog: What way are you thinking to do away with me? To shoot me with the trigger of a gun and to give me shortening of life?

Hazel: The trigger of a gun! God bless it, I never fingered such a thing in the length of my life!

Mineog: To take aim at me and destroy me; to shoot me in forty halves like a crow in the time of the wheat!

Hazel: Oh, now, don't say a thing like that!

Mineog: Or to drown me maybe in the river, enticing me across the rotten plank of the bridge. *(Seizing bottle.)* Will you tell me on the virtue of your oath, is death lurking in that sherry wine?

Hazel: (Pulling out paper.) Ah, God bless your jig! And how would I know is it a notice of my own death has come into my hand in the pocket of this coat I put on me through a mistake?

Mineog: Give it here. That's my property!

Hazel: (Reading.) "We sympathise with Mrs. Hazel and the family." There is proof now. Is it that you would go grieving with my wife and I to be living yet?

Mineog: I didn't follow you out beyond this world with craving for the repose of your soul. It is nothing at all beside what you wrote.

Hazel: Oh, I bear no grudge at all against you. I am not huffy and crabbed like yourself to go taking offence. Sure Kings and big people of the sort are used to see their dead-notices made ready from the hour of their birth out. And it is not anything printed on papers or any flight of words on the *Tribune* could give me any concern at all. See now will I be put out. *(Reads.)* What now is this? "Mr. Hazel was of good race, having in him the old stock of the country, the Mahons, the O'Hagans, the Casserlys——." Where now did you get that? I never heard before, a Casserly to be in my fathers.

Mineog: It might be on the side of the mother.

Hazel: It was not. My mother was a girl of the Hessians that was born in the year of the French. My grandmother was Winefred Kane.

Mineog: What is being out in one name towards drawing down the forecast of all classes of deaths upon myself?

Hazel: There are twenty thousand things you might lay down and I would give them no leave to annoy me. But I have no mind any strange family to be mixed through me, but to go my own road and to carry my own character.

Mineog: I would say you to be very crabbed to be making much of a small little mistake of the sort.

Hazel: I will not have blood put in my veins that never rose up in them by birth. You to have put a slur maybe on the whole of my posterity for ever. That now is a thing out of measure.

Mineog: It might be the Casserlys are as fair as the Hessians, and as well looking and as well reared.

Hazel: There's no one can know that. What place owns them? My tribe didn't come inside the province. Every generation was born and bred in this or in some neighbouring townland.

Mineog: Sure you will be but yourself whatever family may be laying claim to you.

Hazel: Any person of the Casserlys to have done a wrong deed at any time, the neighbours would be watching and probing my own brood till they would see might the track of it break out in any way. It ran through our race to be hard tempered, from the Kanes that are very hot.

Mineog: Why would the family of the Casserlys go doing wrong deeds more than another?

Hazel: I would never forgive it, if it was the highest man in Connacht said it.

Mineog: I tell you there to be any flaw in them, it would have worked itself out in yourself ere this.

Hazel: Putting on me the weight of a family I never knew or never heard the name of at all. It is that is killing me entirely.

Mineog: Neither did I ever hear their name or if they ever lived in the world, or did any deed good or bad in it at all.

Hazel: What made you drag them hither for to write them in my genealogies so?

Mineog: I did not drag them hither——Give me that paper. *(Takes MS. and looks at it.)* What would it be but a misprint? Hessian, Casserly. There does be great resemblance in the sound of a double S.

Hazel: Whether or no, you have a great wrong done me! The person I had most dependence on to be the most person to annoy me! If it was a man from the County Mayo I wouldn't see him treated that way!

Mineog: Have sense now! What would signify anything might be wrote about you, and the green scraws being over your head?

Hazel: That's the worst! I give you my oath I would not go miching from death or be in terror of the sharpness of his bones, and he coming as at the Flood to sweep the living world along with me, and leave no man on earth having penmanship to handle my deeds, or to put his own skin on my story!

Mineog: Ah it's likely the both of us will be forgotten and our names along with us, and we out in the meadow of the dead.

Hazel: I will not be forgotten! I have posterity will put a good slab over me. Not like some would be left without a monument, unless it might be the rags of a cast waistcoat would be put on sticks in a barley garden, to go flapping at the thieves of the air.

Mineog: Let the birds or the neighbours go screech after me and welcome, and I not in it to hear or to be annoyed.

Hazel: Why wouldn't we hear? I'm in dread it's too much I'll hear, and you yourself sending such news to travel abroad, that there is blood in me I concealed through my lifetime!

Mineog: What you are saying now has not the sense of reason.

Hazel: Tom Mineog to say that of me, that was my trusty comrade and my friend, what at all will strangers be putting out about me?

Mineog: Ah, what call have you to go lamenting as if you had lost all on this side of the sea!

Hazel: You to have brought that annoyance on me, what would enemies be saying of me? That it was in my breed to be cracked or to have a thorn in the tongue. There's a generation of families would be great with you, and behind you they would be backbiting you.

Mineog: They will not. You are of a family doesn't know how to say a wrong word.

Hazel: A rabbit mushroom they might say me to be, with no memory behind or around me!

Mineog: Not at all. The world knows you to be civil and brought up to mannerly ways.

Hazel: They might say me to have been a foreigner or a Jew man!

Mineog: I can bear witness you have no such yellow look. And Hazel is a natural name.

Hazel: It's likely they'll say I was a sheep-stealer or a tinker that went foraging around after food!

Mineog: You that never put your hand on a rabbit burrow or stood before a magistrate or a judge!

Hazel: They'll put me down as a grabber that was ready to quench a widow's fire!

Mineog: Oh, where are you running to at all my dear man!

Hazel: And I not to be able at that time to rise up and to get satisfaction! I to be wandering as a shadow and to see some schemer spilling out his lies! That would be the most grief in death! I to hit him a blow of my fist and he maybe not to feel it or to think it to be but a breeze of wind!

Mineog: You are going too far entirely!

Hazel: I to give out a strong curse on him and on his posterity and his land. It would kill my heart if he would take it to be no human voice, but some vanity like the hissing of geese!

Mineog: I myself would recognise your voice, and you to be living or dead.

Hazel: You say that now. But my ghost to come calling to you in the night time to rise up and to clear my character, you would run shivering to the priest as from some unnatural thing. You would call to him to come banish me with a Mass!

Mineog: The Lord be between us and harm.

Hazel: To have no power of revenge after death! My strength to go nourish weeds and grass! A lie to be told and I living I could go lay my case before the courts. So I will too! I'll silence you! I'll learn you to have done with misspellings and with death notices! I'll hinder you bringing in Casserlys! I go take advice from the lawyer! *(Goes towards door.)*

Mineog: I'll go lay down my own case and the way that you have my life threatened!

Hazel: I'll get justice and a hearing. The Judge will give in to my say!

Mineog: I that will put you under bail! I'll bind you over to quit prophesying!

Hazel: I'll break the bail of the sun and moon before I'll give you leave to go brand me with strange names the same as you would tarbrand a sheep! I'll put yourself and your *Tribune* under the law of libel!

Mineog: I'll make a world's wonder of you! I'll give plenty and enough to the *Champion* to fill out its windy pages that time!

Hazel: (At door.) I will lay my information before you will overtake me!

Mineog: (Seizing him.) I will lay my information against you for theft and you bringing away my coat!

Hazel: I have no intention of bringing it away!

Mineog: Is it that you will deny it? Don't I know that spot of grease on the sleeve?

Hazel: Did I never carve a goose? Why wouldn't there be a spot of grease on my own sleeve?

Mineog: Strip it off of you this minute!

Hazel: Give me back my own coat, so!

Mineog: What are you talking about! That's a great wonder now. So it is not my own coat.

Hazel: Strip it off before you will quit the room!

Mineog: I'll be well pleased casting it off!

Hazel: You will not cast it on the dust and the dirt of the floor! *(Helps him.)* Go easy now.——That's it——

(Takes it off gently and places it on chair.)

Mineog: Give me now my own coat!

Hazel: (Struggling with it.) It fails me to get it off.

Mineog: What way did you get it on?

Hazel: It is that it is made too narrow.

Mineog: No, but yourself that has too much bulk.

Hazel: (Struggling.) There now is a tear!

Mineog: (Taking his arm.) Mind now, you'll have it destroyed.

Hazel: Give me a hand, so.

Mineog: (Helping him gently.) Have a care—it's a bit tender in the seams——give me here your hand—it is caught in the rip of the lining.

John: (Coming in, puts pie on table.) Wait now, sir, till I'll aid you to handle Mr. Hazel's coat.

(Whips off coat, takes up other coat, hangs both on pegs.)

The apple pie, Sir.

(Hazel sits down, gasping and wiping his face. Mineog turns his back.)

John: Is there anything after happening, Mr. Hazel?

Hazel: There is not—unless some sort of a battle.

John: Ah, what signifies? There to be more of battles in the world there would be less of wars.

(He pushes Mineog's chair to table.)

Hazel: (After a pause.) Apple pie?

Mineog: (Sitting down.) Indeed, I am not any way inclined for eating.

(Takes plate. John stuffs a cushion into window pane and picks up MSS.)

John: Are these belonging to you, Mr. Mineog?

Mineog: Let you throw them on the coals of the fire, where we have no use for them presently.

Hazel: (Stopping John and taking them.) Thursday is very near at hand. Two empty columns is a large space to go fill.

Mineog: Indeed I am feeling no way fit to go writing columns.

Hazel: (Putting his MS. in his pocket.) There is nothing ails them only to begin a good way after the start, and to stop before the finish.

Mineog: (Putting his MS. in his pocket.) We'll do that. We can put such part of them as we do not need at this time back in the shelf of the press.

Hazel: (Filling glasses and lifting his.) That it may be long before they will be needed!

Mineog: (Lifting glass.) That they may *never* be needed!*Curtain*

DAMER'S GOLD

A COMEDY IN TWO ACTS

PERSONS

Patrick Kirwan CALLED DAMER *Staffy Kirwan* HIS BROTHER *Delia Hessian* HIS SISTER *Ralph Hessian* HER HUSBAND *Simon Niland* THEIR NEPHEW

DAMER'S GOLD

ACT I

Scene: The kitchen in Damer's house. Outer door at back. Door leading to an inner room to right. A dresser, a table, and a couple of chairs. An old coat and hat hanging on the wall. A knocking is heard at door at back. It is unlatched from outside. Delia comes in.

Delia: (Looking round cautiously and going back to door.) You may come in, Staffy and Ralph. There would seem to be no person here.

Staffy: Take care would Damer ask us to cross the threshold at all. I would not ask to go pushing on him, but to wait till he would call to us himself. He is not an easy led man.

Delia: (Crossing and knocking at inner door.) He is not in it. He is likely slipped out unknownst.

Ralph: Herself that thought to find him at the brink of death and nearing his last leap, after what happened him with the jennet. We heard tell of it as far as we were.

Delia: What ailed him to go own a jennet, he that has means to stable a bay horse would set the windows rattling on the public road, and it sparkling over the flintstones after dark?

Staffy: Sure he owns no fourfooted beast only the dog abroad in its box. To make its way into the haggard the jennet did, the time it staggered him with a kick. To forage out some grazing it thought to do, beyond dirt and scutchgrass among the stones. Very cross jennets do be, as it is a cross man it met with.

Delia: A queer sort of a brother he is. To go searching Ireland you wouldn't find queerer. But as soon as I got word what happened I bade Ralph to put the tacklings on the ass. We must have nature about us some way. There was silence between us long enough.

Ralph: She was thinking it might be the cause of him getting his death sooner than God has it promised to him, and that it might turn his mind more friendly like towards us, he knowing us to be at hand for to settle out his burying.

Delia: Why wouldn't it, and we being all the brothers and sisters ever he had, since Jane Niland, God rest her soul, went out last Little Christmas from the troubles and torments of the world.

Staffy: There is nothing left of that marriage now, only one young lad is said to be mostly a fool.

Delia: It is ourselves can bear witness to that, where he came into the house ere yesterday, having no way of living, since death and misfortune scattered him, but as if he was left down out of the skies.

Ralph: He has not, unless the pound piece the mother put into his hand at the last. It is much she had that itself. The time Tom Niland died from her, he didn't leave her hardly the cat.

Staffy: The lad to have any wit around him he would have come travelling hither along with yourselves, to see would he knock any kindness out of Damer.

Ralph: It is what herself was saying, it would be no advantage to him to be coming here at all, he being as he is half light, where there is nothing only will or wit could pick any profit out of Damer. She did not let on to him what side were we facing, and we travelling out from Loughtyshassy.

Staffy: It is likely he will get tidings as good as yourself. It is said, and said largely, Damer has a full gallon jar of gold.

Ralph: There is no one could lift it—God bless it—they were telling me. Filled up it is and brimmed to the very brink.

Staffy: His heart and his soul gone into it. He is death on that gallon of gold.

Delia: He would give leave to the poorhouse to bury him, if he could but put in his will they should leave it down with his bones.

Staffy: A man could live an easy life surely and that much being in the house.

Delia: There is no more grasping man within the four walls of the world. A strange thing he turning to be so ugly and prone to misery, where he was reared along with myself. I have the first covetous person yet to meet I would like! I never would go thrusting after gold, I to get all Lord Clanricarde's estate.

Ralph: She never would, only at a time she might have her own means spent and consumed.

Staffy: The house is very racked beside what it was. The hungriest cabin in the whole ring of Connemara would not show out so empty and so bare.

Delia: (Taking up a jug.) No sign in this vessel of anything that would leave a sign. I'll go bail he takes his tea in a black state, and the milk to be rotting in the churn.

Ralph: (Handling a coat and hat hanging on a nail.) That's a queer cut of a hat. That now should have been a good top-coat in its time.

Delia: For pity's sake! That is the top-coat and the hat he used to be wearing and he riding his long-tailed pony to every racecourse from this to the Curragh of Kildare. A good class of cloth it should be to last out through seventeen years.

Staffy: The time he was young and fundless he had not a bad reaching hand. He never was thrifty but lavish till he came into the ownership of the land. It is as if his luck left him, he growing timid at the time he had means to lose.

Delia: Every horse he would back at that time it would surely win all before it. I saw the people thronging him one time, taking him in their arms for joy, and the winnings coming into his hand. It is likely they ran out through the fingers as swift nearly as they flowed in.

Staffy: He grew to be very dark and crabbed from the time of the father's death. His mind was on his halfpenny ever since.

Delia: (Looking at dresser.) Spiders' webs heaped in ridges the same as windrows in a bleach of hay. What now is that there above on the upper shelf?

Ralph: (Taking it from top shelf.) It is but a pack of cards.

Staffy: They should maybe be the very same that brought him profit in his wild days. He always had a lucky hand.

Delia: (Dusting them.) You would give your seven oaths the dust to have been gathering on them since the time of the Hebrews' Flood. I'll tell you now a thing to do. We being here before him in the house, why wouldn't we ready it and put some sort of face upon it, the way he would be in humour with us coming in.

Ralph: And the way he might incline to put into our hand some good promise or some gift.

Delia: (Dusting.) I would wish no gift from any person at all, but that my mind is set at this time on a fleet of white goats and a guinea-hen are to be canted out from the Spanish woman at Lisatuwna cross by reason of the hanging gale.

Staffy: That was the way with you, Delia, from the time you could look out from the half-door, to be coveting pictures and fooleries, that would shape themselves in your mind.

Delia: There is no sin coveting things are of no great use or profit, but would show out good and have some grandeur around them. Those goats now! Browsing on the blossoms of the bushes they would be, or the herbs that give out a sweet smell. Stir yourself, Staffy, and throw your eye on that turf beyond in the corner. It is that wet you could wring from it splashes and streams. Let you rise the ashes from the sods are on the hearth and redden them with a goosewing, if there is a goosewing to be found. There is no greater beauty to be met with than the leaping of a little yellow flame.

Staffy: In my opinion there will no pay-day come for this work, but only a thank-you job; a County Clare payment, 'God spare you the health!'

Delia: Let you do it, Ralph so. *(Takes potatoes from a sieve.)* A roasted potato would be a nice thing to put before him, in the place of this old crust of a loaf. Put them in now around the sods, the way they will be crispy before him.

Ralph: (Taking them.) And the way he will see you are a good housekeeper and will mind well anything he might think fit to give.

Delia: (At clock.) I'll set to the right time of day the two hands of the clock are pointing a full hour before the sun. Take, Staffy, that pair of shoes and lessen from them the clay of the land. That much of doing will not break your heart. He will be as proud as the fallen angels seeing the way we have all set out before him.

(A harsh laugh is heard at inner door. They turn and see Damer watching them.)

Ralph: Glory be to God!

Delia: It is Damer was within all the time!

Staffy: What are you talking about, Delia? It is Patrick you were meaning to say.

Damer: Let her go on prattling out Damer to my face, as it is often she called it behind my shoulders. Damer the chandler, the miser got the spoil of the Danes, that was mocked at since the time of the Danes. I know well herself and the world have me christened with that nickname.

Ralph: Ah, it is not to dispraise you they put it on you, but to show you out so wealthy and so rich.

Damer: I am thinking it is not love of my four bones brings you on this day under my thatch?

Staffy: We heard tell you were after being destroyed with a jennet.

Damer: Picking up newses and tidings of me ye do be. It is short the delay was on you coming.

Delia: And I after travelling through the most of the day on the head of you being wounded and hurt, thinking you to be grieving to see one of your own! And I in dread of my life stealing past your wicked dog.

Damer: My joy he is, scaring you with his bark! If it wasn't for him you would have me clogged and tormented, coming in and bothering me every whole minute.

Delia: There is no person in Ireland only yourself but would have as much welcome for me to-day as on the first day ever they saw me!

Damer: What's that you are doing with my broom?

Delia: To do away with the spider's webs I did, where the shelves were looped with them and smothered. Look at all that came off of that pack of cards.

Damer: What call had you to do away with them, and they belonging to myself? Is it to bleed to death I should and I to get a tip of a billhook or a slasher? You and your vagaries to have left me bare, that I would be without means to quench the blood, and it to rise up from my veins and to scatter on every side!

Delia: Is it that you are without e'er a rag, and that ancient coat to be hanging on the wall?

Damer: The place swept to flitters! What is that man of yours doing and he handling my turf?

Ralph: It was herself thought to be serviceable to you, setting out the fuel that was full of dampness where it would get an air of the fire.

Damer: To dry it is it? *(Seizes sods and takes them from the hearth.)* And what length would it be without being burned and consumed and it not to be wet putting it on? *(Pours water over it.)* And I after stacking it purposely in the corner where there does be a drip from the thatch.

Ralph: She but thought it would be more answerable to you being dry.

Damer: What way could I bear the expense of a fire on the hearth and it to leave smouldering and to break out into a blaze? A month's cutting maybe to go to ashes within three minutes, and into wisps of smoke. And the price of turf in this year gone wild out of measure, and it packed so roguish you could read the printed speeches on the paper through the sods you do be buying in the creel.

Staffy: I was saying myself not to meddle with it. It is hurry is a worse friend than delay.

Damer: Where did you get those spuds are roasting there upon the hearth?

Ralph: Herself that brought them out from the sieve, thinking to make ready your meal.

Damer: My seed potatoes! Samples I got from the guardians and asked in the shops and in stores till I'd gather enough to set a few ridges in the gardens would serve me through the length of the year!

Delia: Let you be satisfied so with your mouldy bit of loaf. *(Breaks a bit from it and hands it to him.)*

Damer: Do not be breaking it so wasteful! The mice to have news there was as much as that of crumbs in the house, they would be running the same as chickens around the floor!

Ralph: Thinking to be comfortable to you she was, the way you would make us welcome from this out.

Damer: Which of ye is after meddling with my clock?

Delia: It was a full hour before its time.

Darner: It to be beyond its time, wouldn't that save fire and candles sending me to my bed early in the night? Leave down those boots! *(Takes them from Staffy.)* Is it that you are wearing out the uppers with scraping at them and scratching! Is it to rob me ye are come into this place?

Delia: I tell you we only came in getting word that you were done and dying.

Damer: Ha! Is it to think I was dying ye did? Well, I am not. I am not so easy quenched. Strength and courage I have, to keep a fast grip of what I own.

Delia: Let you not be talking that way! We are no grabbers and no thieves!

Damer: I have it in my mind that ye are. Very ravenous to run through my money ye are.

Delia: The world knows I am not ravenous! I never gave my heart to silver or to gold but only to the thing it would bring in. But to hold from me the thing my heart is craving after, you might as well blacken the hearth.

Damer: Striving to scare me out of my courage and my wits, the way I'll give in to go making my will.

Ralph: She would not be wishful you to do that the time your mind would be vexed.

Damer: I'll make it, sick or sound, if I have a mind to make it.

Delia: Little thanks you'll get from me if you make it or do not make it. That is the naked truth.

Damer: The whole of ye think yourselves to be very managing and very wise!

Delia: Let you go will it so to an asylum for fools.

Damer: Why wouldn't I? It is in the asylums all the sense is these times. There is only the fools left outside.

Delia: You to bestow it outside of your own kindred for to benefit and comfort your soul, all the world will say it is that you had it gathered together by fraud.

Staffy: Do not be annoying him now.

Delia: I will not. But the time he will be lying under the flagstone, it is holly rods and brambles will spring up from out of his thorny heart.

Damer: A hasty, cranky woman in the house is worse than you to lay your hand upon red coals! I know well your tongue that is as sharp as the sickle of the moon!

Delia: The character you will leave after you will be worse out and out than Herod's!

Damer: The devil upon the winds she is! That one was born into the world having the use of the bow and arrows!

Delia: You not to give fair play to your own, it is a pitiful ghost will appear in your image, questing and craving our prayers!

Damer: I know well what is your aim and your drift!

Delia: I say any man has a right to give thanks to the heavens, and he having decent people to will his means to, in place of people having no call to it.

Damer: Whoever I'll will it to will have call to it!

Delia: Or to part with it to low people and to mean people, and you having it to give.

Damer: Having it to give is it? Do you see that lock on the door?

Delia: I do see it and have eyes to see it. .

Damer: Can you make any guess what is inside of it?

Delia: It is likely it is what there is so much talk about, your own full gallon of gold.

(Ralph takes off his hat.)

Damer: Lay now your eye to that lock hole.

Ralph: *(Looking through keyhole.)* It is all dusky within. It fails me to see any shining thing.

(Staffy and Delia put their eyes to keyhole but draw back disappointed.)

Darner: If you cannot see it, try can you get the smell of it. Take a good draw of it now; lay your head along the hinges of the door. So now ye may quit and scamper out of this, the whole throng of ye, robbers and hangmen and bankbreakers, bargers and bad characters, and you may believe me telling you that is the nearest ye ever will come to my gold!

(He bangs back into room locking door after him.)

Delia: He has no more nature than the brutes of the field, hunting and howling after us.

Staffy: Yourself that rose him out of his wits and his senses. We will sup sorrow for this day's work where he will put curses after us. It is best for us go back to my place. It may be to-morrow that his anger will be cured up.

Ralph: I thought it was to lay him out with candles we were brought here. I declare I came nearer furnishing out a corpse myself with the start I got.

Delia: There is no dread on me. When he gets in humour I will tackle up again to him. It is too far I came to be facing back to Loughtyshassy and I fasting from the price of my goats! Little collars I was thinking to buckle around their neck the same as a lady's lapdog, and maybe so far as a small clear-sounding bell.

(They go out, Damer comes back. He puts on clock, rakes out fire, picks up potatoes and puts them back in sieve, takes bread into his room. There is a knock at the door. Then it is cautiously opened and Simon Niland comes in, and stands near the hearth. Damer comes back and sees him.)

Damer: What are you looking for?

Simon: For what I won't get seemingly, that is a welcome.

Damer: Maybe it's for fists you are looking?

Simon: It is not, before I will get my rest. I couldn't box to-night if I was the Queen of England.

Damer: Have you any traffic with that congregation is after going out?

Simon: I seen no person good or bad, but a dog and it on the chain.

Damer: You to have in you any of the breed of the Kirwans that is my own, I'd rise the tongs and pitch you out from the door!

Simon: I suppose you would not begrudge me to rest myself for a while, *(Sits down.)*

Damer: I'll give leave to no strolling vagabond to sit in any place at all.

Simon: All right so.
(Tosses a coin he takes from his pocket, tied in a spotted handkerchief.)

Damer: What's that you're doing?

Simon: Pitching a coin I was to see would it bid me go west or east.

Damer: Go toss outside so.

Simon: *(Stooping and groping.)* I will after I will find it.

Damer: Hurry on now.

Simon: Wait till I'll kindle a match. *(Lights one and picks up coin.)*

Damer: What is that in your hand?

Simon: You should know.

Damer: Is it gold it is?

Simon: It is all I have of means in the world. I never handled a coin before it, but my bite to be given me and my bed.

Damer: You'll mind it well if you have sense.

Simon: It is towards the east it bade me go. I'll travel as far as the races of Knockbarron to-morrow.

Damer: You'll be apt to lose it going to races.

Simon: I'll go bet with it, and see what way will it turn out.

Damer: You to set all you own upon a horse that might fail at the leaps! It is a very foolish thing doing that.

Simon: It might not. Some have luck and are born lucky and more have run through their luck. If I lose it, it is lost. It would not keep me long anyway. I to win, I will have more and plenty.

Damer: You will surely lose it.

Simon: If I do I have nothing to get or to fall back on. It is some other one must take my charges.

Damer: A great pity to go lose a gold sovereign to some schemer you never saw before.

Simon: Sure you must take some risk. You cannot put your hands around the world.

Damer: It to be swept by a trick of the loop man!

Simon: It is not with that class I will make free.

Damer: To go lose the whole of it in one second of time!

Simon: I will make four divides of it.

Damer: To go change it into silver and into copper! That would be the most pity in the world.

Simon: I'll chance it all upon the one jock so.

Damer: Gold! Believe me it is a good thing to hold and a very heartbreak the time it is lost. *(Takes it in his hand.)* Pure gold! There is not a thing to be got with it as worthy as what it is itself! There is no comfort in any place and it not in it. The Queen's image on it and her crown. Solid between the fingers; weighty in the palm of the hand; as beautiful as ever I saw.

Simon: It is likely it is the same nearly as any other one.

Damer: Gold! My darling it is! From the hollows of the world to the heights of the world there is no grander thing to be found. My bone and my marrow! Let me have the full of my arms of it and I'll not ask the flowers of field or fallow or the dancing of the Easter sun!

Simon: I am thinking you should be Damer. I heard said Damer has a full crock of gold.

Damer: He has not! He has not!

Simon: That is what the world says anyway. I heard it as far as the seaside.

Damer: I wish to my God it was true!

Simon: Full and brimming to the brink. That is the way it was told.

Damer: It is not full! It is not! Whisper now. It is many a time I thought it to be full, full at last, full at last!

Simon: And it wasn't after?

Damer: To take it and to shake it I do. It is often I gave myself a promise the time there will be no sound from it, I will give in to nourish myself, I will rise out of misery. But every time I will try it, I will hear a little clatter that tells me there is some space left; some small little hole or gap.

Simon: What signifies that when you have so much in it?

Damer: Weightier it gets and weightier, but there will always be that little sound. I thought to stop it one time, putting in a fistful of hayseed; but I felt in my heart that was not dealing fair and honest with myself, and I rose up and shook it out again, rising up from my bed in the night time. I near got my death with the cold and the draught fell on me doing that.

Simon: It is best for me be going on where I might find my bed,

Damer: Hearken now. I am old and the long road behind me. You are young and in your strength. It is you is rich, it is I myself that is poor. You know well, you to get the offer, you would not change your lot with my own.

Simon: I suppose I might not. I'd as lief keep my countenance and my run.

Darner: Isn't it a great pity there to be that hollow within in my gallon, and the little coin that would likely just fill it up, to be going out of the house?

Simon: Is it that you are asking it of me?

Damer: You might never find so good a way to open Heaven to yourself with a charity. To be bringing peace to an old man that has not long to live in the world! You wouldn't think now how quiet I would sleep, and the good dreams would be going through me, and that gallon jar to be full and to make no sound the time I would roll it on the floor. That would be a great deed for one little pound piece to do!

Simon: I'll toss you for it.

Damer: I would not dare put anything at all upon a chance.

Simon: Leave it alone so. *(Turns away.)*

Damer: *(Seizing him.)* It would make such a good appearance in the little gap!

Simon: Head or harp?

Damer: No, I'm in dread I might lose.

Simon: Take your chance or leave it.

Damer: I to lose, you may kill me on the moment! My heart is driven down in the sole of my shoe!

Simon: That is poor courage.

Damer: There is some shiver forewarning me I will lose! I made a strong oath I never would give in again to try any sort of chance.

Simon: You didn't make it but with yourself.

Damer: It was through my luck leaving me I swore against betting and gaming.

Simon: It might turn back fresh and hearty where you gave it so long a rest.

Damer: Well—maybe——

Simon: Here now.

Damer: I dare not.

Simon: (Going to door.) I'll make my bet so according to a dream I had. It is on a red horse I will put it to-morrow.

Damer: No—stop—wait a minute.

Simon: I'll win surely following my dream.

Damer: I might not lose.

Simon: I'm in dread of that. All turns to the man is rich.

Damer: I'll chance it!

Simon: You said no and I'll take no.

Damer: You cannot go back of your word.

Simon: Let me go out from you tempting me.

Damer: (Seizing him.) Heads! I say heads!

Simon: Harps it is. I win.

Damer: My bitter grief! Ochone!

Simon: I'll toss you for another.

Damer: You will not. What's tosses? Look at here what is put in my way! *(Holds up pack of cards.)*

Simon: Where's the stakes?

Damer: Wait a second. *(Goes into room.)*

Simon: Hurry on or I won't stop.

Damer: Let you not stir out of that!
(Comes back and throws money on table.)

Simon: Come on so.
(Shuffles cards.)

Darner: Give me the pack. *(Cuts.)* I didn't feel a card between my fingers this seven and a half-score years!

Simon: Spades are trumps.

Darner: *(Lighting candle.)* I'll win it back! I won't begrudge spending a penny candle, no, or two penny candles! I'll play you to the brink of day!

Curtain

ACT II

The next morning. The same kitchen. Simon Niland is lying asleep on the hearth. Ralph and Staffy are looking at him.

Staffy: Who is it at all is in it?

Ralph: Who would it be but Simon Niland, that is come following after us.

Staffy: Stretched and sleeping all the same as if there was a pin of slumber in his hair, as in the early times of the world. The day passing without anything doing. That one will never win to a fortune.

Ralph: It would be as well for ourselves maybe he not to be too great with Damer.

Staffy: Will Delia make any headway I wonder. She had good courage to go face him, and he abroad on the land, sitting stooped on the bent body of a bush.

Ralph: I wonder what way did that lad make his way into this place. Wait now till I'll waken and question him.

(Shakes Simon.)

Simon: *(Drowsily.)* Who is that stirring me?

Ralph: Rouse yourself up now.

Simon: Do not be rousing me, where I am striving to catch a hold of the tail of my last dream.

Staffy: Is it seeking for a share of Damer's wealth you are come?

Simon: I never asked and never looked for it.

Staffy: You are going the wrong road to reach to it.

Simon: A bald cat there was in the dream, was keeping watch over jewelleries in a cave.

Staffy: No person at all would stretch out his hand to a lad would be rambling and walking the world, and it in its darkness and sleep, and be drowsing and miching from labour through the hours the sun has command of.

Delia: (At the door). Is it that ye are within, Staffy and Ralph?

Ralph: We are, and another along with us.

Delia: Put him out the door!

Ralph: Ah, there's no danger of him coming around Damer. He is simple and has queer talk too.

Delia: Put him out I say! *(Pushes Simon to door.)* Let him drowse out the day in the car shed! I tell you Damer is at hand!

Ralph: Has he the frown on him yet?

Staffy: Did his anger anyway cool down?

Delia: He is coming I say. I am partly in dread of him. I am afeard and affrighted!

Ralph: He should be in terrible rages so. There was no dread on you yesterday, and he cursing and roaring the way he was.

Delia: He is mad this time out and out. Wait now till you'll see!

(She goes behind dresser. Damer comes to the door. Staffy goes behind a chair. Ralph seizes a broom.)

Damer: (At door.) Are you acquainted with any person, Ralph Hessian, is in need of a savage dog?

Staffy: Is it that you are about to part Jubair your dog?

Damer: I have no use for him presently.

Staffy: Is it that you are without dread of robbers coming for to knock in your skull with a stone? Or maybe out in the night it is to burn you out of the house they would.

Damer: What signifies, what signifies? All must die, all must die. The longest person that will live in the world, he is bound to go in the heel. Life is a long road to travel and a hard rough track under the feet.

Staffy: Mike Merrick the huckster has an apple garden bought against the harvest. He should likely be seeking for a dog. There do be little lads passing to the school.

Damer: He might want him, he might want him. *(He leans upon half-door.)*

Staffy: Is it that you are tired and wore out carrying the load of your wealth?

Damer: It is a bad load surely. It was the love of money destroyed Buonaparte where he went robbing a church, without the men of learning are telling lies.

Staffy: I would never go so far as robbery, but to bid it welcome I would, and it coming fair and easy into my hand.

Damer: There was a king out in Foreign went astray through the same sin. His people that made a mockery of him after his death, filling up his jaws with rendered gold. Believe me, any person goes coveting after riches puts himself under a bad master.

Staffy: That is a master I'd be willing to engage with, he to give me my victuals and my ease.

Damer: In my opinion it was to keep temptation from our path the gold of the world was covered under rocks and in the depths of the streams. Believe me it is best leave it where it is, and not to meddle with the Almighty.

Staffy: You'd be best without it. It is the weight of it is bowing you to your grave. When things are vexing your mind and you are trouble minded they'll be going through your head in the night time. There is a big shift and a great change in you since yesterday. There is not the half of you in it. You have the cut of the misfortune.

Damer: I am under misfortune indeed.

Staffy: Give over now your load to myself before the coming of the dusk. The way you are there'll be nothing left of you within three days. There is no way with you but death.

Delia: (To Ralph.) Let you raise your voice now, and come around him on my own behalf.

Ralph: It is what herself is saying, you to be quitting the world as it seems, it is as good for you make over to her your crock of gold.

Damer: I would not wish, for all the glories of Ireland, to leave temptation in the path of my own sister or my kin, or to twist a gad for their neck.

Delia: (To Ralph.) Tell him I'll chance it.

Damer: At the time of the judgment of the mountain, when the sun and moon will be all one with two blackberries, it is not being pampered with plenty will serve you, beside being great with the angels!

Delia: (Shrinking back.) I would as soon nearly not get it at all, where it might bring me to the wretched state of Damer! *(Dog heard barking.)*

Damer: I'll go bring my poor Jubair out of this. A great sin and a great pity to be losing provision with a dog, and the image of the saints maybe to be going hungry and bare. How do I know what troop might be bearing witness against me before the gate of heaven? To be cherishing a ravenous beast might be setting his teeth in their limbs! To give charity to the poor is the best religion in Ireland. Didn't our Lord Himself go beg through three and thirty years? *(He goes.)*

Delia: (Coming forward.) Will you believe me now telling you he is gone unsteady in the head?

Staffy: I see no other sign. He is a gone man surely. His understanding warped and turned backward. To see him blighted the way he is would stir the heart of a stone.

Ralph: He surely got some vision or some warning, or there lit on him a fit or a stroke.

Staffy: Twice a child and only once a man. He is turned to be innocent with age.

Ralph: It would be a bad thing he to meet with his death unknown to us.

Delia: It would be worse again he that is gone out of his latitude to be brought away to the asylum.

Ralph: I don't know.

Delia: But I know. He to die, and to make no will, it is ourselves, by rule and by right, that would lay claim to his wealth.

Staffy: So we could do that, and he to come to his end in the bad place, God save the mark!

Delia: Would you say there would be no fear the Government might stretch out and take charge of it, saying him to be outside of his reason?

Ralph: That would be the worst of all. We to be forced to hire an attorney against them, till we would break one another at law.

Delia: He to be stopping here, and being light in the brain, it is likely some thief travelling the road might break his way in and sweep all.

Ralph: It would be right for us keep some sort of a watch on it.

Staffy: What way would we be sitting here watching it, the same as a hen on a pebble of flint, through a quarter or it might be three quarters of a year? He might drag for a good while yet, and live and linger into old days.

Delia: To take some cross turn he might, and to come at us violent and maybe tear the flesh from our bones.

Staffy: It is best for us do nothing so, but to leave it to the foreknowledge of God.

Delia: There is but the one thing to do. To bring it away out of this and to lodge it within in my own house. We can settle out a place under the hearth.

Staffy: We can make a right division of it at such time as the end will come.

Ralph: What way now will we bring away the crock?

Delia: Let you go outside and be watching the road while Staffy will be bringing out the gold.

Staffy: Ah, I'm not so limber as what Ralph is. There does be giddiness and delay in my feet. It might fail me to heave it to a hiding place and to bring it away unknownst.

Delia: Let you go out so and be keeping a watch, and Ralph will put it on the ass-car under sacks.

Ralph: Do it you. I am not of his own kindred and his family. Any person to get a sketch of me bringing it away they might nearly take myself to be a thief.

Delia: We are doing but what is fair and is right.

Ralph: Maybe so. But any neighbour to be questioning me, it might be hard put a skin on the story.

Delia: There is no person to do it but the one. *(Calls from the door.)* Come in here from the shed, Simon Niland, if the sluggishness is banished from your eyesight and from your limbs.

Simon: (At door) I was thinking to go travel my road.

Delia: Have you any desire to reach out your hand for to save a mortal life?

Simon: (Coming in.) Whose life is that?

Staffy: The man of this house that is your uncle and is owner of wealth closed up in a jar. We now being wittier than himself, that has lost his wits, have our mind made up to bring it away.

Simon: Outside of his knowledge is it?

Staffy: It will be safe and well minded and lodged in loyal keeping, it being no profit to him that is at this time shook and blighted, but only a danger to his days.

Delia: The seven senses to be going astray on him, what would ail any tramp or neuk that would be passing the road, not to rob him and to lay him stone dead?

Staffy: Go in now and bring out from the room and to such place as we will command, that gallon jar of gold.

Ralph: It being certain it will be brought away from him, it is best it to be kept in the family, and not to go nourishing lawyers or thieves.

Simon: Is it to steal it I should?

Staffy: What way will it be stealing, and the whole of us to be looking on at your deed?

Simon: Ah, what call have I to do that much and maybe put myself in danger of the judge, for the sake of a man is without sense.

Delia: Let you do it for my own sake so. You heard me giving out news on yesterday of the white goats are on the bounds of being sold. The neighbours will give me no more credit, where they loaned me the price of a crested side car was auctioned out at a quality sale.

Ralph: Picking the eyes out of my own head they are, to pay the little bills they have against her.

Delia: I am no way greedy, I would ask neither food or bite, I would not begrudge turning Sunday into Friday if I could but get my heart's desire. Such a thing now as a guinea-hen would be bringing fashion to the door, throwing it a handful of yellow meal, and it in its speckled plumage giving out its foreign call!

Simon: I have no mind to be brought within the power of the law.

Delia: You that are near in blood to refuse me so small an asking, what chance would I have sending requests to Heaven that is beyond the height of the clouds!

(Weeps.)

Staffy: That's the way with them that are reared poor, they are the hardest after to humour, striving to bring everything to their own way. But there's a class of people in the world wouldn't do a hand's turn, no more than the bird upon the tree.

Ralph: I wonder you not to give in to us, when all the world knows God formed young people for to be giving aid to elder people, and beyond all to them that are near to them in blood.

Staffy: Look now, Simon, let you be said and led by me. You having no great share of wisdom we are wishful to make a snug man of you and to put you on a right road. Go in now and you will not be kept out of your own profit and your share, and a harbour of plenty beyond all.

Simon: It might be guarded by a serpent in a tree, or by unnatural things would be in the similitude of cats.

Staffy: Ah, that class is done away with this good while.

Ralph: There is no person having sense, but would take means, by hook or by crook, to make his pocket stiff and he to be given his fair chance. It is to save you from starvation we are wishful to do, as much as to bring profit to ourselves.

Staffy: You not to follow our say you will be brought to burn green ferns to boil your victuals, or to devour the berries of the bush.

Simon: I would not wish a head to follow me and leap up on the table and wrestle me, or to drink against me with its gory mouth.

Staffy: You that have not the substance of a crane's marrow, to go shrink from so small a bidding, let you go on the shaughraun or to the workhouse, where you would not take our advice.

Simon: I'll go do your bidding so. I will go bring out the crock.

Staffy: There is my whiteheaded boy! I'll keep a watch, the way Damer will not steal in on us without warning.

Ralph: He should have the key in some secret place. It is best for you give the lock a blow of your foot.

Simon: I'll do that.
(He gives door a kick. It opens easily.)

Delia: Was I right now saying Damer is turned innocent? Sure the door was not locked at all.

Simon: (Dragging out jar.) Here it is now.

Ralph: So it is and no mistake.

Staffy: There should be great weight in it.

Ralph: I am in dread it might work a hole down through the timber of the car.

Delia: Why wouldn't we open it here? It would be handier bringing it away in small divides.

Ralph: The way we would make sure of getting our own share at the last.

Delia: Let you draw out the cork from it.

Ralph: I don't know can I lift it. *(Stoops and lifts it easily.)* The Lord protect and save us! There is no weight in it at all!

Staffy: *(Seizing and shaking it.)* Not a one penny in it but clean empty. That beats all.

Delia: It is with banknotes it is stuffed that are deaf and do be giving out no sound. *(She pokes in a knitting pin.)* Nothing in it at all, but as bare as the canopy of heaven!

Ralph: There being nothing within in it, where now is the gold?

Staffy: Some person should have made away with it.

Delia: Some robber or some great rogue. A terrible thing such ruffians to be around in the world! To turn and rob a poor man of all he had spared and had earned.

Staffy: They have done him a great wrong surely, taking from him all he had of comfort in his life.

Ralph: My grief it is there being no more hangings for thieves, that are worse again than murderers that might do their deed out of heat. It is thieving is the last crime.

Staffy: We to lay our hand on that vagabond we'll give him cruelty will force him to Christian habits.

Ralph: Take care might he be nearer than what you think! *(He points at Simon. All look at him.)*

Staffy: Sure enough it is with himself only we found him on the hearth this morning.

Delia: He hasn't hardly the intellect to be the thief.

Simon: I tell you I never since the day I was born could be charged with the weight of a brass pin!

Staffy: It is to Damer, my fine boy, you will have to make out your case.

Simon: So I will make it out. Where now is Damer?

Staffy: He is gone down the road, where he brought away Jubair the dog.

Simon: What are you saying? The dog gone is it? *(Goes to door.)*

Ralph: (Taking hold of him.) What makes you go out in such a hurry?

Simon: What is that to you?

Delia: What cause has he to be making a run?

Simon: Let me mind my own business.

Staffy: It is maybe our own business.

Simon: To make a search I must in that dog's kennel of straw.

Delia: Go out, Ralph, till you will bring it in.

(Ralph goes out.)

Staffy: (Seizing him) A man to go rush out headlong and money after being stolen, I have no mind to let him make his escape.

Delia: If you are honest let you stop within and not to put a bad appearance upon yourself making off.

Simon: Let me out! I tell you I have a thing concealed in the box.

Staffy: A strange place to go hiding things and a queer story altogether.

Delia: Do not let go your hold. He to go out into the street, he has the wide world before him.

Ralph: (Dragging kennel in.) Here now is the box.

Simon: (Breaking away and searching it) Where at all is it vanished?

Staffy: It is lies he was telling. There is nothing at all within in it only a wisp of barley straw.

Simon: Where at all is it?

Staffy: What is it is gone from you?

Simon: Not a one pound left!

Delia: Why would you look to find coins of money down in Jubair's bed?

Simon: It is there I hid it.

Staffy: What is it you hid?

Simon: All that was in the crock and that I took from it. Where now is my bag of gold?

Staffy: Do you hear what he is after saying?

Ralph: A lad of that sort will not be safe but in the gaol. Let us give him into the grip of the law.

Delia: No, but let the man owned it do that.

Staffy: So he can task him with it, and he drawing to the door.

Delia: (Going to it.) It is time for you, Patrick, come in.

(Damer comes in dragging a sack.)

Ralph: You are after being robbed and left bare.

Delia: Not a one penny left of all you have cast into its mouth.

Ralph: Herself made a prophecy you would be robbed with the weakening of your wits, and sure enough it has come about.

Delia: Not a tint of it left. What now do you say, hearing that?

Damer: (Sitting down by the hearth and laying down sack.) If it should go it must go. That was allotted to me in the skies.

Delia: Is it that you had knowledge ere this of it being swept and lost?

Damer: If I had not, why would I have been setting my mind upon eternity and striving to bring to mind a few prayers? And to have parted with my wicked dog?

Delia: Let you turn around till you will see before you the man that is the robber and the thief!

Simon: Thief yourself! You that had a plan made up to bring it away.

Damer: Delia, Delia, what was I laying down a while ago? It is the love of riches has twisted your heart and your mind.

Delia: Is it that you are contented to be made this one's prey?

Damer: It was foretold for me, I to go stint the body till I near put myself to death without the Lord calling on me, and to lose every whole pound after in one night's card playing.

Delia: Is it at cards you lost it?

Damer: With that same pack of cards you laid out under my hand, I lost all I had gathered to that one.

Staffy: Well, there is nothing so certain in the world as the running of a fool to a fool.

Delia: Is it taking that lad you are to be a fool? I thinking him to be as simple as you'd see in the world, and he putting bread upon his own butter as we slept!

Ralph: We to have known all then we know now, we need not have wasted on him our advice.

Damer: Give me, boy, one answer. What in the world wide put venture into you that made you go face the dog?

Simon: Ah, what venture? And he being as he is without teeth?

Damer: You know that, what no one in the parish or out of it ever found out till now! You should have put your hand in his jaw to know that much! A right lad you are and a lucky lad. I would nearly wish you of my own blood and of my race.

Delia: Of your own blood is it?

Damer: That is what I would wish.

Delia: Is it that you are taking Simon Niland to be a stranger?

Damer: What Simon Niland?

Delia: Your own nephew and only son to your sister Sarah.

Damer: Do you tell me so! What way did it fail me to recognise that, and he having daring and spirit the same as used to be rising up in myself in my early time?

Delia: He was born the very year of you coming into possession of this place.

Damer: The same year my luck turned against me, and every horse I would back would get the staggers on the course, or would fail to rise at the leaps. All the strength of fortune went from me at that time, it is into himself it flowed and ran. The dead spit and image of myself he is. Stop with me here through the winter season and through the summer season! You to be in the house it is not an unlucky house will be in it. The Royalty of England and of Spain cannot touch upon yourself. I am prouder of you than if you wrote the wars of Homer or put down Turgesius of the Danes! You are a lad that can't be beat. It is you are the Lamb of Luck!

Staffy: What call has he or any of us to be stopping under Damer's roof and he owning but the four walls presently and a poor little valley of land?

Ralph: There is nothing worth while in his keeping, and all he had gathered after being robbed.

Damer: Is that what you are saying? Well, I am not so easy robbed as you think! *(Takes bag from the sack and shakes it.)* Is that what you call being robbed?

Simon: That is my treasure and my bag!

Staffy: I thought it was after being brought away from the two of you.

Damer: You are out of it! It is Jubair did that much for me. Jubair, my darling, it is tonight I'll bring him back to the house! It is not in the box he will be any more but alongside the warmth of the hearth. The time I went unloosing his chain, didn't he scrape with his paw till he showed me all I had lost hid in under the straw, and it in a spotted bag! *(Opens and pours out money.)*

Simon: It is as well for you have it back where it stopped so short with myself.

Damer: Is it that I would keep it from you where it was won fair? It is a rogue of a man would do that. Where would be the use, and I knowing you could win it back from me at your will, and the five trumps coming into your hand? It is to share it we will and share alike, so long as it will not give out!

Delia: A little handsel to myself would do the both of you no harm at all.

Damer: Delia, my darling, I'll go as far as that on this day of wonders. I'll handsel you and welcome. I'll bestow on you the empty jar. *(Gives it to her.)*

Delia: I'll take it. I'll let on it to be weighty and I facing back into Loughtyshassy.

Ralph: The neighbours seeing it and taking you to be his heir you might come to your goats yet.

Delia: Ah, what's goats and what is guinea-hens? Did ever you see yoked horses in a coach, their skin shining out like shells, rising their steps in tune the same as a patrol of police? There are peacocks on the lawns of Lough Cutra they were telling me, having each of them a hundred eyes. *(Goes to door.)*

Simon: (Putting his hand on the jar.) I don't know. *(To Damer)* It might be a nice thing for the two of us to start gathering the full of it again.

Damer: Not a fear of me. Where heaping and hoarding that much has my years withered and blighted up to this, it is not to storing treasure in any vessel at all I will give the latter end of my days, or to working the skin off my bones. Give me here that coat. *(Puts it on.)* If I was tossed and racked a while ago I'll show out good from this out. Come on now, out of this, till we'll face to the races of Loughrea and of Knockbarron. I was miserable and starved long enough. *(Puts on hat.)* I'm thinking as long as I'll be living I'll take my view of the world, for it's long I'll be lying when my eyes are closed and seeing nothing at all!

(He seizes a handful of gold and puts it in Simon's pocket and another in his own. They turn towards the door.)

Curtain

McDONOUGH'S WIFE

PERSONS

McDonough, a piper. First Hag. Second Hag.

McDONOUGH'S WIFE

Scene: A very poor room in Galway with outer and inner door. Noises of a fair outside. A Hag sitting by the fire. Another standing by outer door.

First Hag: Is there e'er a sign of McDonough to be coming?

Second Hag: There is not. There were two or three asking for him, wanting him to bring the pipes to some spree-house at the time the fair will be at an end.

First Hag: A great wonder he not to have come, and this the fair day of Galway.

Second Hag: He not to come ere evening, the woman that is dead must go to her burying without one to follow her, or any friend at all to flatten the green scraws above her head.

First Hag: Is there no neighbour at all will do that much, and she being gone out of the world?

Second Hag: There is not. You said to ask Pat Marlborough, and I asked him, and he said there were plenty of decent women and of well-reared women in Galway he would follow and welcome the day they would die, without paying that respect to one not belonging to the district, or that the town got no good account of the time she came.

First Hag: Did you do as I bade you, asking Cross Ford to send in a couple of the boys she has?

Second Hag: What a fool I'd be asking her! I laid down to her the way it was. McDonough's wife to be dead, and he far out in the country, and no one belonging to her to so much as lift the coffin over the threshold of the door.

First Hag: What did she say hearing that?

Second Hag: She put a big laugh out of her, and it is what she said: "May the devil die with her, and it is well pleased the street will be getting quit of her, and it is hard say on what mountain she might be grazing now."

First Hag: There will no help come burying her so.

Second Hag: It is too lofty McDonough was, and too high-minded, bringing in a woman was maybe no lawful wife, or no honest child itself, but it might be a bychild or a tinker's brat, and he giving out no account of her generations or of her name.

First Hag: Whether or no, she was a little giddy. But that is the way with McDonough. He is sometimes an unruly lad, but he would near knock you with his pride.

Second Hag: Indeed he is no way humble, but looking for attendance on her, as if she was the youngest and the greatest in the world.

First Hag: It is not to humour her the Union men will, and they carrying her to where they will sink her into the ground, unless it might be McDonough would come back, and he having money in his hand, to bring in some keeners and some hired men.

Second Hag: He to come back at this time it is certain he will bring a fist-full of money.

First Hag: What makes you say that to be certain?

Second Hag: A troop of sheep-shearers that are on the west side of the fair, looking for hire from the grass farmers. I heard them laying down they met with McDonough at the big shearing at Cregroostha.

First Hag: What day was that?

Second Hag: This day week for the world.

First Hag: He has time and plenty to be back in Galway ere this.

Second Hag: Great dancing they had and a great supper at the time the shearing was at an end and the fleeces lodged in the big sacks. It is McDonough played his music through the night-time. It is what I heard them saying, "He went out of that place weightier than he went in."

First Hag: He is a great one to squeeze the pipes surely. There is no place ever he went into but he brought the whip out of it.

Second Hag: His father was better again, they do be saying. It was from the other side he got the gift.

First Hag: He did, and from beyond the world, where he befriended some in the forths of the Danes. It was they taught him their trade. I heard tell, he to throw the pipes up on top of the rafters, they would go sounding out tunes of themselves.

Second Hag: He could do no more with them than what McDonough himself can do—may ill luck attend him! It is inhuman tunes he does be making; unnatural they are.

First Hag: He is a great musician surely.

Second Hag: There is no person can be safe from him the time he will put his "come hither" upon them. I give you my word he set myself dancing reels one time in the street, and I making an attack on him for keeping the little lads miching from school. That was a great scandal to put upon a decent woman.

First Hag: He to be in the fair to-day and to take the fancy, you would hear the nailed boots of the frieze-coated man footing steps on the sidewalk.

Second Hag: You would, and it's likely he'd play a notion into the skulls of the pampootied boys from Aran, they to be kings of France or of Germany, till they'd go lift their head to the clouds and go knocking all before them. And the police it is likely laughing with themselves, as if listening to the talk of the blackbird would be perched upon a blessed bush.

First Hag: I wonder he did not come. Could it be he might be made away with for the riches he brought from Cregroostha? It would be a strange thing now, he to be lying and his head broke, at the butt of a wall, and the woman he thought the whole world of to be getting her burial from the workhouse.

(A sound of pipes.)

Second Hag: Whist, I tell you! It's the sound of the pipes. It is McDonough, it is no other one.

First Hag: (Getting up.) I'm in dread of him coming in the house. He is a hasty man and wicked, and he vexed. What at all will he say and she being dead before him? Whether or no, it will be a sharp grief to him, she to scatter and to go. He might give me a backstroke and drive me out from the door.

Second Hag: Let you make an attack upon himself before he will have time to make his own attack.

McDonough: (Coming in.) Catherine! Where is she? Where is Catherine?

First Hag: Is it readying the dinner before you, or wringing out a shirt for the Sunday like any good slave of a wife, you are used to find your woman, McDonough?

McDonough: What call would she have stopping in the house with the withered like of yourself? It is not to the crabbed talk of a peevish hag a handsome young woman would wish to be listening and sport and funning being in the fair outside.

First Hag: Go look for her in the fair so, if it is gadding up and down is her habit, and you being gone out from her sight.

McDonough: (Shaking her.) Tell me out, where is she?

First Hag: Tell out what harbour were you yourself in from the day you left Cregroostha?

McDonough: Is it that she got word?—or that she was tired waiting for me?

First Hag: She is gone away from you, McDonough.

McDonough: That is a lie, a black lie.

First Hag: Throwing a lie in a decent woman's face will not bring you to the truth.

McDonough: Is it what you are laying down that she went away with some other man? Say that out if you have courage, and I'll wring your yellow windpipe.

First Hag: Leave your hand off me and open the room door, and you will see am I telling you any lie.

McDonough: (Goes to door, then stops.) She is not in it. She would have come out before me, and she hearing the sound of the pipes.

First Hag: It is not the sound of the pipes will rouse her, or any sound made in this world at all.

McDonough: (Trembling.) What is it?

First Hag: She is gone and she is not living.

McDonough: Is it to die she did? *(Clutches her.)*

First Hag: Yesterday, and the bells ringing, she turned her face to the south and died away. It was at the hour of noon I knew and was aware she was gone. A great loss it to be at the time of the fair, and all the lodgers that would have come into the house.

McDonough: It is not truth. What would ail her to die?

First Hag: The makings of a child that came before its time, God save the mark! She made a bad battle at the last.

McDonough: What way did it fail you to send me out messengers seeking me when you knew her to be done and dying?

First Hag: I thought she would drag another while. There was no time for the priest itself to overtake her, or to put the little dress of the Virgin in her hand at the last gasp of death.

McDonough goes into the room. He comes out as if affrighted, leans his head against the wall, and breaks into a prayer in Irish:

"An Athair tha in Naomh, dean trocaire orainn! A Dia Righ an Domhain, dean trocaire orainn! A Mhuire Mathair Dia, dean trocaire orainn!"

Second Hag: (Venturing near.) Do not go fret after her, McDonough. She could not go through the world forever, and travelling the world. It might be that trouble went with her.

McDonough: Get out of that, you hags, you witches you! You croaking birds of ill luck! It is much if I will leave you in the living world, and you not to have held back death from her!

Second Hag: That you may never be cross till you will meet with your own death! What way could any person do that?

McDonough: Get out the door and it will be best for you!

Second Hag: You are talking fool's talk and giving out words that are foolishness! There is no one at all can put away from his road the bones and the thinness of death.

McDonough: I to have been in it he would not have come under the lintel! Ugly as he is and strong, I would be able for him and would wrestle with him and drag him asunder and put him down! Before I would let him lay his sharp touch on her I would break and would crush his naked ribs, and would burn them to lime and scatter them!

First Hag: Where is the use raving? It is best for you to turn your hand to the thing has to be done.

McDonough: You to have stood in his path he might have brought you away in her place! That much would be no great thing to ask, and your life being dead and in ashes.

First Hag: Quieten yourself now where it was the will of God. She herself made no outcry and no ravings. I did my best for her, laying her out and putting a middling white sheet around her. I went so far as to smoothen her hair on the two sides of her face.

McDonough: (Turning to inner door.) Is it that you are gone from me, Catherine, you that were the blossom of the branch!

(Old woman moans.)

It is a bad case you to have gone and to have left me as lonesome after you as that no one ever saw the like!

(The old woman moans after each sentence.)

I to bring you travelling you were the best traveller, and the best stepper, and the best that ever faced the western blast, and the waves of it blowing from you the shawl! I to be sore in the heart with walking you would make a smile of a laugh. I would not feel the road having your company; I would walk every whole step of Ireland.

I to bring you to the dance-house you would dance till you had them all tired, the same in the late of the day as in the commencement! Your steps following quick on one another the same as hard rain on a flagstone! They could not find your equal in all Ireland or in the whole ring of Connemara!

What way did it fail me to see the withering of the branches on every bush, as it is certain they withered the time laughter died with your laugh? The cold of winter has settled on the hearth. My heart is closed up with trouble!

First Hag: It is best for us shut the door and to keep out the noises of the fair.

McDonough: Ah, what sort at all are the people of the fair, to be doing their bargaining and clutching after their luckpenny, and she being stark and quiet!

First Hag: She has to be buried ere evening. There was a messenger of a clerk came laying that down.

McDonough: May ill luck attend him! Is it that he thinks she that is gone has no person belonging to her to wake her through the night-time?

First Hag: He sent his men to coffin her. She will be brought away in the heel of the day.

McDonough: It is a great wake I will give her. It would not be for honour she to go without that much. Cakes and candles and drink and tobacco! The table of this house is too narrow. It is from the neighbours we should borrow tables.

First Hag: That cannot be. It is what the man said, "This is a common lodging-house. It is right to banish the dead from the living." He has the law with him, and custom. There is no use you thinking to go outside of that.

McDonough: My lasting grief it will be I not to get leave to show her that respect!

First Hag: "There will a car be sent," he said, "and two boys from the Union for to bear her out from the house."

McDonough: Men from the Union, are you saying? I would not give leave to one of them to put a hand anigh or anear her! It is not their car will bring her to the grave. That would be the most pity in the world!

First Hag: You have no other way to bring her on her road. It is best for you give in to their say.

McDonough: Where are the friends and the neighbours that they would not put a hand tinder her?

First Hag: They are after making their refusal. She was not well liked in Galway. There is no one will come to her help.

McDonough: Is that truth, or is it lies you have made up for my tormenting?

First Hag: It is no lie at all. It is as sure as the winter's frost. You have no one to draw to but yourself.

McDonough: It is mad jealous the women of Galway were and wild with anger, and she coming among them, that was seventeen times better than their best! My bitter grief I ever to have come next or near them, or to have made music for the lugs or for the feet of wide crooked hags! That they may dance to their death to the devil's pipes and be the disgrace of the world! It is a great slur on Ireland and a great scandal they to have made that refusing! That the Corrib River may leave its merings and rise up out of its banks till the waves will rise like mountains over the town and smother it, with all that is left of its tribes!

First Hag: Be whist now, or they will be angered and they hearing you outside in the fair.

McDonough: Let their day not thrive with the buyers and the sellers in the fair! The curse of mildew on the tillage men, that every grain of seed they have sowed may be rotten in the ridges, and the grass corn blasted from the east before the latter end of harvest! The curse of the dead on the herds driving cattle and following after markets and fairs! My own curse on the big farmers slapping and spitting in their deal! That a blood murrain may fall upon their bullocks! That rot may fall upon their flocks and maggots make them their pasture and their prey between this and the great feast of

Christmas! It is my grief every hand in the fair not to be set shaking and be crookened, where they were not stretched out in friendship to the fair-haired woman that is left her lone within boards!

Second Hag: (At door.) Is it a niggard you are grown to be, McDonough, and you with riches in your hand? Is it against a new wedding you are keeping your pocket stiff, or to buy a house and an estate, that it fails you to call in hired women to make a right keening, and a few decent boys to lift her through the streets?

McDonough: I to have money or means in my hand, I would ask no help or be beholden to any one at all.

Second Hag: If you had means, is it? I heard by true telling that you have money and means. "At the sheep-shearers' dance a high lady held the plate for the piper; a sovereign she put in it out of her hand, and there was no one of the big gentry but followed her. There never was seen so much riches in any hall or home." Where now is the fifty gold sovereigns you brought away from Cregroostha?

McDonough: Where is it?

Second Hag: Is it that you would begrudge it to the woman is inside?

McDonough: You know well I would not begrudge it.

First Hag: A queer thing you to speak so stiff and to be running down all around you, and your own pocket being bulky the while.

McDonough: (Turning out pocket.) It is as slack and as empty as when I went out from this.

Second Hag: You could not have run through that much.

McDonough: Not a red halfpenny left, or so much as the image of a farthing.

First Hag: Is it robbed and plundered you were, and you walking the road?

McDonough: (Sitting down and rocking himself.) I wish to my God it was some robber stripped and left me bare! Robbed and plundered! I was that, and by the worst man and the unkindest that ever was joined to a woman or lost a woman, and that is myself.

First Hag: Is it to lose it unknownst you did?

McDonough: What way did I lose it, is it? I lost it knowingly and of my own will. Thrown on counters, thrown on the drink-house floor, given for spirits, given for porter, thrown for drink for friends and acquaintances, for strangers and strollers and vagabonds. Scattered in the parish of Ardrahan and at Labane cross. Tramps and schemers lying drunk and dead drunk at the butt of every wall. *(Buries head in his hands.)*

First Hag: That is what happened the gold yourself and the pipes had won? You made no delay doing that much. You have a great wrong done to the woman inside, where you left her burying bare.

Second Hag: She to be without a farthing dip for her corpse, and you after lavishing gold.

First Hag: You have a right to bruise your knees making repentance, you that lay on the one pillow with her. You to be putting curses upon others and making attacks on them! I would make no complaint, you to be naked at your own burying and at the very hour of death, and the rain falling down on your head.

McDonough: Little I mind what happens me. There is no word you can put out of your mouth can do me any injury at all. Oh, Catherine, it is best for me go hang myself out of a tree, and my carcass to be torn by savage dogs that went famished through a great length of time, and my bones left without a token or a flag or a headstone, and my name that was up at one time to be forgotten out of mind! *(He bursts out sobbing.)*

First Hag: The shadows should be lengthening in the street. Look out would you see the car to be coming.

Second Hag: It was a while ago at the far corner of the fair. They were but waiting for the throng to lessen.

First Hag: They are making too much delay.

Second Hag: I see a hint of the livery of the poorhouse coming through the crowd.

First Hag: The men of the Union are coming to bring her away, McDonough. There is nothing more to be done. She will get her burial from the rates.

McDonough: Oh, Catherine, Catherine! Is it I myself have brought you to that shame and that disgrace!

Second Hag: You are making too much of it. Little it will signify, and we to be making clay, who was it dug a hole through the nettles or lifted down the sods over our head.

First Hag: That is so. What signifies she to be followed or to be going her lone, and her eyes being shut to the world?

McDonough: Is that the thought ye have within ye, ye Galway hags? It is easy known it is in a trader's town you were bred, and in a street among dealers.

First Hag: I was but saying it does not signify.

McDonough: But I say it does signify! I will tell that out to you and the world! That might be the thought of a townsman or a trader, or a rich merchant itself that had his estate gained by trafficking, for that is a sort does be thinking more of what they can make out of the living than of keeping a good memory of the dead!

First Hag: There are worthier men than yourself, maybe, in storehouses and in shops.

McDonough: But I am of the generations of Orpheus, and have in me the breed of his master! And of Raftery and Carolan and O'Daly and all that made sounds of music from this back to the foundations of the earth! And as to the rich of the world, I would not humble my head to them. Let them have their serving men and their labourers and messengers will do their bidding. But the servant I myself command is the pipes that draws its breath from the four winds, and from a wind is beyond them again, and at the back of the winds of the air. She was a wedded woman and a woman having my own gold ring on her hand, and my own name put down with hers in the book. But she to have been a shameless woman as ye make her out to be, and sold from tinker to tinker on the road it is all one! I will show Galway and the world that it does signify; that it is not fitting McDonough's wife to travel without company and good hands under her and good following on the road. Play now, pipes, if you never played before! Call to the keeners to follow her with screams and beating of the hands and calling out! Set them crying now with your sound and with your notes, as it is often you brought them to the dance-house!

(Goes out and plays a lament outside.)

First Hag: (Looking out.) It is queer and wild he is, cutting his teeth and the hair standing on him.

Second Hag: Some high notion he has, calling them to show honour to her as if she was the Queen of the Angels.

First Hag: To draw to silence the whole fair did. Every person is moving towards this house.

(A murmur as of people. McDonough comes in, stands at door, looking out.)

McDonough: I squeeze the pipes as a challenge to the whole of the fair, gentle noble and simple, the poor and the high up. Come hither and cry Catherine McDonough, give a hand to carry her to the grave! Come to her aid, tribes of Galway, Lynches and Blakes and Frenches! McDonough's pipes give you that command, that have learned the lamentation of the Danes.

Come follow her on the road, trades of Galway, the fishermen, and the carpenters, and the weavers! It is by no short road we will carry her that never will walk any road from this out! By Williams-gate, beside Lynch's gallows, beside the gaol of the hangings, the salmon will make their leap as we pass!

Men at Door: We will. We will follow her, McDonough.

Others: Give us the first place.

Others: We ourselves will carry her!

McDonough: Faith, Catherine, you have your share and your choice this day of fine men, asking to carry you and to lend you their strength.

I will give no leave to traffickers to put their shoulder under you, or to any that made a refusal, or any seaside man at all.

I will give leave to no one but the sheep-shearers from Eserkelly, from Moneen and Cahirlinny and the whole stretch of Cregroostha. It is they have friendship for music, it is they have a wish for my four bones.

(Sheep-shearers come in. They are dressed in white flannel. Each has a pair of shears at his side. The first carries a crook.)

First Sheep-shearer: Is it within there she is, McDonough?

First Hag: Go in through the door. The boards are around her and a clean quilt over them. Have a care not to leave down your hands on it, and they maybe being soiled with the fair.

(They take off their hats and go in.)

McDonough: (Turning to her door.) If you got no great honour from your birth up, and went barefoot through the first of your youth, you will get great respect now and will be remembered in the times to come.

There is many a lady dragging silk skirts through the lawns and the flower knots of Connacht, will get no such grand gathering of people at the last as you are getting on this day.

It is the story of the burying of McDonough's wife will be written in the book of the people!

(Sheep-shearers appear at inner door. McDonough goes out, squeezing the pipes. Triumphant music is heard from outside.)

Curtain

NOTES

THE BOGIE MEN

A message sent to America from Dublin that our Theatre had been "driven out with hisses"; an answering message from New York that the *Playboy*, the cause of battle, was now "as dead as a doornail," set me musing with renewed delight on our incorrigible genius for myth-making, the faculty that makes our traditional history a perpetual joy, because it is, like the Sidhe, an eternal Shape-changer.

At Philadelphia, the city of trees, where in spite of a day in the police court and before a judge, and the arrest of our players at the suit not of a Puritan but a publican, and the throwing of currant cake with intent to injure, I received very great personal kindness, a story of his childhood told by my host gave me a fable on which to hang my musings; and the Dublin enthusiast and the American enthusiast who interchanged so many compliments and made so brave a show to one another, became Dermot and Timothy, "two harmless drifty lads," the *Bogie Men* of my little play. They were to have been vagrants, tatterdemalions, but I needed some dress the change of which would change their whole appearance in a moment, and there came to mind the chimney sweepers of my childhood.

They used to come trotting the five miles from Loughrea, little fellows with blue eyes shining out from soot-black faces, wearing little soot-coloured smocks. Our old doctor told us he had gone to see one of them who was sick, and had found him lying in a box, with soot up to his chin as bedding and blanket.

Not many years ago a decent looking man came to my door, with I forget what request. He told me he had heard of ghosts and fairies, but had never met with anything worse than himself, but that he had had one great fright in his lifetime. Its cause had been the squealing and outcry made by two rats caught in one trap, that had come clattering down a flight of steps one time when he was a little lad, and had come sweeping chimneys to Roxborough.

[Music: AIR OF "ALL AROUND MY HAT I WILL WEAR A GREEN RIBBON!"]

THE FULL MOON

It had sometimes preyed on my mind that *Hyacinth Halvey* had been left by me in Cloon for his lifetime, bearing the weight of a character that had been put on him by force. But it failed me to release him by reason, that "binds men to the wheel"; it took the call of some of those unruly ones who give in to no limitations, and dance to the sound of music that is outside this world, to bring him out from "roast and boiled and all the comforts of the day." Where he is now I do not know, but anyway he is free.

Tannian's dog has now become a protagonist; and Bartley Fallon and Shawn Early strayed in from the fair green of *Spreading the News*, and Mrs. Broderick from the little shop where *The Jackdaw* hops on the counter, as witnesses to the miracle that happened in Hyacinth's own inside; and it is likely they may be talking of it yet; for the talks of Cloon are long talks, and the histories told there do not lessen or fail.

As to Davideen's song, I give the air of it below. The Queen Anne in it was no English queen, but, as I think, that Aine of the old gods at whose hill mad dogs were used to gather, and who turned to grey the yellow hair of Finn of the Fianna of Ireland. It is with some thought of her in their mind that the history-tellers say "Anne was not fair like the Georges but very bad and a tyrant. She tyrannised over the Irish. She was very wicked; oh! very wicked indeed!"

[Music: AIR OF "THE HEATHER BROOM!"]

COATS

I find some bald little notes I made before writing *Coats*. "Hazel is astonished Mineog can take such a thing to heart, but it is quite different when he himself is off ended." "The quarrel is so violent you think it can never be healed, but the ordinary circumstances of life force reconciliation. They are the most powerful force of all." And then a quotation from Nietzsche, "A good war justifies every cause."

DAMER'S GOLD

In a lecture I gave last year on playwriting I said I had been forced to write comedy because it was wanted for our theatre, to put on at the end of the verse plays, but that I think tragedy is easier. For, I said, tragedy shows humanity in the grip of circumstance, of fate, of what our people call "the thing will happen," "the Woman in the Stars that does all." There is a woman in the stars they say, who is always hurting herself in one way or other, and according to what she is doing at the hour of your birth, so will it happen to you in your lifetime, whether she is hanging herself or drowning herself or burning herself in the fire. "And," said an old man who was telling me this, "I am thinking she was doing a great deal of acting at the time I myself made my start in the world." Well, you put your actor in the grip of this woman, in the claws of the cat. Once in that grip you know what the end must be. You may let your hero kick or struggle, but he is in the claws all the time, it is a mere question as to how nearly you will let him escape, and when you will allow the pounce. Fate itself is the protagonist, your actor cannot carry much character, it is out of place. You do not want to know the character of a wrestler you see trying his strength at a show.

In writing a little tragedy, *The Gaol Gate*, I made the scenario in three lines, "He is an informer; he is dead; he is hanged." I wrote that play very quickly. My two poor women were in the clutch of the Woman in the Stars.... I knew what I was going to do and I was able to keep within those three lines. But in comedy it is different. Character comes in, and why it is so I cannot explain, but as soon as one creates a character, he begins to put out little feet of his own and take his own way.

I had been meditating for a long time past on the mass of advice that is given one by friends and well-wishers and relations, advice that would be excellent if the giver were not ignorant so often of the one essential in the case, the one thing that matters. But there is usually something out of sight, of which the adviser is unaware, it may be something half mischievously hidden from him, it may be that "secret of the heart with God" that is called religion. In the whole course of our work at the theatre we have been I may say drenched with advice by friendly people who for years gave us the reasons why we did not succeed.... All their advice, or at least some of it, might have been good if we had wanted to make money, to make a common place of amusement. Our advisers did not see that what we wanted was to create for Ireland a theatre with a base of realism, with an apex of beauty. Well, last summer I made a fable for this meditation, this emotion, at the back of my mind to drive.

I pictured to myself, for I usually first see a play as a picture, a young man, a mere lad, very sleepy in the daytime. He was surrounded by people kind and wise, who lamented over his rags and idleness and assured him that if he didn't get up early and do his work in the daytime he would never know the feel of money in his hand. He listens to all their advice, but he does not take it, because he knows what they do not know, that it is in the night time precisely he is filling his pocket, in the night when, as I think, we receive gifts from the unseen. I placed him in the house of a miser, an old man who had saved a store of gold. I called the old man Damer, from a folk-story of a chandler who had bought for a song the kegs of gold the Danes had covered with tallow as a disguise when they were driven out of Ireland, and who had been rich and a miser ever after. I did not mean this old man, Damer, to appear at all. He was to be as invisible as that Heaven of which we are told the violent take it by force. My intention at first was that he should be robbed, but then I saw robbery would take too much sympathy from my young lad, and I decided the money should be won by the lesser sin of cardplaying, but still behind the scenes. Then I thought it would have a good stage effect if old Damer could just walk once across the stage in the background. His relations might have come into the house to try and make themselves agreeable to him, and he would appear and they would vanish. ... Damer comes in, and contrary to my intention, he begins to find a tongue of his own. He has made his start in the world, and has more than a word to say. How that play will work out I cannot be sure, or if it will ever be finished at all. But if ever it is I am quite sure it will go as Damer wants, not as I want.

That is what I said last winter, and now in harvest time the play is all but out of my hands. But as I foretold, Damer has taken possession of it, turning it to be as simple as a folk-tale, where the innocent of the world confound the wisdom of the wise. The idea with which I set out has not indeed quite vanished, but is as if "extinct and pale; not darkness, but light that has become dead."

As to Damer's changes of mood, it happened a little time ago, when the play was roughly written, but on its present lines, that I took up a volume of Montaigne, and found in it his justification by high examples:

"Verilie it is not want but rather plentie that causeth avarice. I will speake of mine owne experience concerning this subject. I have lived in three kinds of condition since I came out of my infancie. The first time, which continued well nigh twentie yeares, I have past it over as one who had no other means but casual without any certaine maintenance or regular prescription. My expenses were so much the more carelessly laid out and lavishly employed, by how much more they wholly depended on fortunes rashnesse and exhibition. I never lived so well at ease.... My second manner of life hath been to have monie: which when I had once fingred, according to my condition I sought to hoorde up some against a rainy day.... My minde was ever on my halfe-penny; my thoughts ever that way. Of commoditie I had little or nothing.... And after you are once accustomed, and have fixed your thoughts upon a heape of monie, it is no longer at your service; you dare not diminish it; it is a building which if you touch or take any part from it, you will think it will all fall. And I should sooner pawne my clothes or sell a horse, with lesse care and compulsion than make a breach into that beloved purse which I kept in store.... I was some yeares of the same humour: I wot not what good Demon did most profitably remove me from it, like to the Siracusan, and made me to neglect my sparing.... I live from hand to mouth, from day to day, and have I but to supplie my present and ordinarie needs I am satisfied.... And I singularly gratifie myself this correction came upon me in an age naturally inclined to covetousnesse, and that I am free from that folly so common and peculiar to old men, and the most ridiculous of all humane follies. Feraulez who had passed through both fortunes and found that encrease of goods was no encrease of appetite to eat, to sleepe or to embrace his wife; and who on the other side felt heavily on his shoulders the importunitie of ordering and directing his Oeconomicall affairs as it doth on mine, determined with himselfe to content a poore young man, his faithfull friend, greedily gaping after riches, and frankly made him a present donation of all his great and excessive riches, always provided hee should undertake to entertaine and find him, honestly and in good sort, as his guest and friend. In which estate they lived afterwards most happily and mutually content with the change of their condition."

And so I hope it may come to pass with the remaining years of Simon and of Damer.

McDONOUGH'S WIFE

In my childhood there was every year at my old home, Roxborough, or, as it is called in Irish, Cregroostha, a great sheep-shearing that lasted many days. On the last evening there was always a dance for the shearers and their helpers, and two pipers used to sit on chairs placed on a corn-bin to make music for the dance. One of them was always McDonough. He was the best of all the wandering pipers who went about from house to house. When, at my marriage, I moved from the barony of Dunkellin to the neighbouring barony of Kiltartan, he came and played at the dance given to the tenants in my honour, and he came and played also at my son's coming of age. Not long after that he died. The last time I saw him he came to ask for a loan of money to take the train to Ennis, where there was some fair or gathering of people going on, and I would not lend to so old a friend, but gave him a half-sovereign, and we parted with kindly words. He was so great a piper that in the few years since his death myths have already begun to gather around him. I have been told that his father was taken into a hill of the Danes, the Tuatha de Danaan, the ancient invisible race, and they had taught him all their tunes and so bewitched his pipes that they would play of themselves if he threw them up on the rafters. McDonough's pipes, they say, had not that gift, but he himself could play those inspired tunes. Lately I was told the story I have used in this play about his taking away fifty sovereigns from the shearing at Cregroostha and spending them at a village near. "I said to him," said the old man who told me this, "that it would be better for him to have bought a good kitchen of bacon; but he said, 'Ah, when I want more, I have but to squeeze the pipes.'" The story of his wife's death and burial as I give it has been told to me here and there. That is my fable, and the emotion disclosed by the story is, I think, the lasting pride of the artist of all ages:

"We are the music makers
And we are the dreamers of dreams....
We in the ages lying
In the buried past of the earth
Built Nineveh with our sighing,
And Babel itself with our mirth."

I wrote the little play while crossing the Atlantic in the *Cymric* last September. Since it was written I have been told at Kinvara that "McDonough was a proud man; he never would go to a wedding unasked, and he never would play through a town," So he had laid down pride for pride's sake, at that time of the burying of his wife.

In Galway this summer one who was with him at the end told me he had a happy death, "But he died poor; for what he would make in the long nights he would spend through the summer days." And then she said, "Himself and Reilly and three other fine pipers died within that year. There was surely a feast of music going on in some other place."

Dates of production of plays.

THE BOGIE MEN was first produced at the Court Theatre, London, July 8, 1912, with the following cast:

Taig O'Harragha J. M. KERRIGAN *Darby Melody* J. A. O'ROURKE

THE FULL MOON was first produced at the Abbey Theatre, Dublin, on November 10, 1910, with the following cast:

Shawn Early J. O'ROURKE *Bartley Fallon* ARTHUR SINCLAIR *Peter Tannian* SIDNEY MORGAN *Hyacinth Halvey* FRED. O'DONOVAN *Mrs. Broderick* SARA ALLGOOD *Miss Joyce* EILEEN O'DOHERTY *Cracked Mary* MAIRE O'NEILL *Davideen* J. M. KERRIGAN

COATS was first produced at the Abbey Theatre,
Dublin, December, 1910, with the following cast:

Mineog ARTHUR SINCLAIR *Hazel* J. M. KERRIGAN *John* J. A. O'ROURKE

DAMER'S GOLD was first produced at the Abbey Theatre November 21, 1912, with the following cast:

Delia Hessian SARA ALLGOOD *Staffy Kirwan* SIDNEY MORGAN *Ralph Hessian* J. M. KERRIGAN *Damer* ARTHUR SINCLAIR *Simon Niland* A. WRIGHT

McDONOUGH'S WIFE has not yet been produced by the Abbey Company.